Getting Jobs
Advertising

CASSELL JOB GUIDES

Getting Jobs in Advertising
BY JENNY TIMBER

Getting Jobs in Beauty
BY LESLEY MOORE

Getting Jobs in Fashion Design
BY ASTRID A. KATCHARYAN

Getting Jobs in Graphic Design
BY TERRY JONES

Getting Jobs in Music
BY TONY ATWOOD

Getting Jobs in Photography
BY KIM HOWARD

Getting Jobs in Broadcasting
BY FIONA RUSSELL

Getting Jobs Outdoors
BY MURRAY MARSHALL

Getting Jobs in Advertising

Jenny Timber

CASSELL

Cassell Publishers Limited
Artillery House, Artillery Row
London SW1P 1RT

First published 1988

British Library Cataloguing in Publication Data

Timber, Jenny
Getting jobs in advertising.
1. Advertising – Career guides
I. Title
659.1'023

ISBN 0 304 31481 1

Some occupations, titles, phrases or individual words in this publication
may refer to a worker or workers of a particular sex, but they should not be
taken to imply that the occupation or career is restricted to one sex, unless
the occupation is excluded from the general provisions of the Sex
Discrimination Act

The views expressed in this book are those of the author and not necessarily
those of the Inner London Education Authority.

Typeset by Scribe Design, Gillingham, Kent
Printed and bound in Great Britain by
Billings & Sons Limited, Book Plan, Worcester

Contents

Acknowledgements 7

Why this book? 9
How to use this book 9
How the book is arranged 10
Getting jobs in Advertising 10
A personal note 10

1 The Advertising Business **11**

What is advertising? 11
The advertisers 12
What is marketing? 17
The agencies 18
The media 18
The specialist companies 20

2 Working for an advertiser **24**

Anatomy of an advertiser: the Prudential 25

3 Advertising agencies **32**

How many jobs? 32
Where are the jobs? 33
The Account Executive 34
The Account Planner 37
The Creative Department 38
The Media Department 43
The Production Department 44
What qualities are required? 45
Answers to quiz 46

**4 Anatomy of an agency: Bartle Bogle Hegarty, or how
to get it right** **47**

Account Handler 47
Media Planner/Buyer 49
Copy-writer 51
Accounts Department 53
Client Account Planner 54
Production and Traffic 55

Contents

5 Advertising sales   57

Remember advertising sales   57
Why advertising sales?   57
What sort of people get in?   62
How to get a job   62

**6 Anatomy of an advertising sales department: The
Guardian – Classified Advertising Sales**   63

The Advertising Department   63
Telephone Sales   65
Field and Display Sales   68

7 Getting jobs in advertising   73

Finding the vacancies and getting in   73
Tales of graduate recruitment   80

8 Courses and qualifications   83

Watford College: the copy-writing course   83
Hounslow College   87
CAM Education Foundation   89
BTEC courses, degrees and other 'business' advertising courses   92
The Institute of Marketing's exams   93
Graphic design courses   93
The School of Communications Arts   93
Advertising bodies   94

Useful addresses   95

Further reading   96

Acknowledgements

The author and publishers thank the following for permission to reproduce illustrations:

p. 8   A detail from a Deighton and Mullen advertisement in *World Advertising Review 1988*, published by Cassell;

pp. 14–15, 16   Information in the table from *Campaign's* analysis of MEAL. Persil ads from J. Walter Thompson;

p. 19   Tango;

pp. 20–1   Baker Tamborini Creative Services;

pp. 25, 26, 29   The Prudential;

pp. 40, 41, 48, 50, 53, 59 (bottom)   Bartle Bogle Hegarty Agency;

pp. 64, 66–7, 70   The *Guardian* newspaper;

p. 72   Watford College;

p. 84   Hounslow Borough College students: Mercedes Morgan and James Sexton;

p. 86   Hounslow Borough College students: top, Lorraine Lowe and Teresa Coyne; centre, Richard Dean and Alan Morrice; bottom, Richard Eccleston;

pp. 88, 90   Hounslow Borough College students.

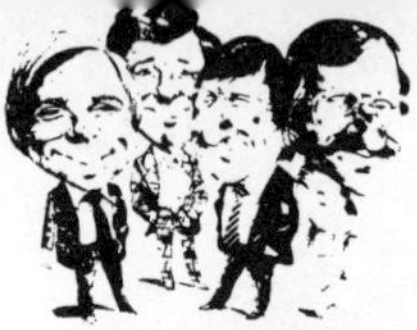

GREGORY/ELLIS/MARTIN & PA

STANLEY DICKS

AAP KETCHUM

The Creative Busin

SLAYMAKER COWLEY WHITE

THE BUCHANAN COMPANY LIMITED

BDG

HCA

LEO BURNETT ADVERTISING

YELLOWHAMMER

Buchanan

INCORPORATED PRACTITIONERS IN ADVERTISING

De Monde Advertising Ltd.

Travis Dal

GARRETT, DOYLE, FUGLER.

EDWARDS MARTIN THORN

LOVELL & RUPERT CURT

DOYLE DANE BERNBACH LIMITED

COGENT ELLIOTT

Y&R

MODULE

Park ADVERTISING AND MARKETING

FCB

SYMINGTON

Collett, Dickenson, Pearce and Par

ASPECT HILL HOLLIDAY

SPEC

Redheads

MILLER + K

DELANEY FLETCH

da Costa & Co ADVERTISING CONSULTANCY

WUNDERMAN

Anderson & Lembke

McK MARKETING

T·R·J

Abraham Ellis & Partners Ltd

LIPPA NEWTON

McCORMICK-PUBLICIS

Riley A

DMB&B

WETHEY · SCOTT · ADVERTISING ·

We apologise to any agencies that have changed their name(s) since the [illegible] campaign. Unfortunately [illegible] went to press. We look forward to seeing their new improved logos.

Why this book?

This book is written for people considering advertising as a career – either as a first job or as a job change. It tells you who the employers are, what the jobs are, how you can get into them and gives you some examples of people who have successfully done this. It also gives you a flavour of the business, so that you can decide if you want to make the effort to get into and succeed in this very competitive world.

People who have decided on advertising as a career and are preparing themselves for applications and interviews will also find this book useful. Advertising agencies expect their potential employees, especially graduates, to have a grasp of what the business is about. Even for school-leavers, applying for very junior jobs, the enthusiastic, well-informed, committed and interested person is the one who gets taken on.

How to use this book

The advertising business, as you can see on page 13, is made up of three main areas: the advertiser, the agency and the media. There are a variety of jobs within these three areas; some with qualifications in common, others requiring special ones for particular jobs. On the whole, educational standards are high: many people have degrees, A-levels or specialist qualifications, but this is by no means universal. There are some notable examples of people in advertising who have got in by talent and hard work rather than by good qualifications.

You may be very definite about your immediate plans – knowing that you are going to university or art school, or leaving school at 16 – or you may be unsure of them. You may be an adult wishing to change your career. You may have some specific sector or job in advertising in mind, or you may be just generally interested at this stage.

Look at the sections which follow. They are designed to pin-point chapters which are of particular interest to you. If you read a chapter and find it is describing something that is not appropriate for you, go back to the Contents page and try some of the alternatives. However, you should also read the whole book – particularly if, after dipping in, you decide you are seriously interested.

How the book is arranged

Each general section is followed by an example. For instance, the advertising sales chapter is followed by a chapter on advertising sales at the *Guardian*.

The general section is designed to give you an accurate, overall picture of the business. The examples are to give you a more specific flavour. Bear in mind that an example is just that – other agencies will not be exactly the same as Bartle Bogle Hegarty, and it would be tedious to read about six. Always refer to the general sections and do not jump to conclusions from the examples.

Getting jobs in Advertising

Finding your way into a career can be difficult. Sometimes it's difficult because, although there's a clear way in, there are more people than openings, and it's very competitive. Sometimes it's difficult because no one is sure what the way in is, and people need advice and help to get their first job in that career.

Both these difficulties apply to advertising. There are some ways in that are very clear (the graduate-recruitment schemes of the large agencies, for example), and competitive. The ways in for other jobs (copy-writing, for example), or for people in other situations (school-leavers), are not so clear and more careful explanation is needed to help people break in.

A personal note

I have been dealing with careers in advertising for many years. During this time I've talked to large numbers of young people wanting to get in, and to equally large numbers of employers. It seemed a waste not to put down all I've learned in a book, so that it could be useful to more people.

Quite apart from offering an informative and advisory book, I hope you find it a good read. Advertising is a fascinating and complex business, and even if you decide in the end it isn't for you it's still interesting to know about it. If you decide it is for you and you want to go on with your application, then good luck and, more importantly, work hard!

The Advertising Business

Before you read this chapter, ask yourself two very simple questions:

1. What is marketing?
2. What is advertising?

Write down your answers and look at them again when you've finished the chapter.

What is advertising?

The reply that people usually make to this question is that it's to do with selling something. It is indeed. Of course, 'the something' is not necessarily soap powder or cornflakes, which are the usual products people associate with advertising. It could be a service, such as those provided by a bank, or British Rail; or it could be something much more vague, such as the image of a corporation, like British Petroleum; or it could be a point of view, for example, the one of a particular political party. In some campaigns, the selling could be called educating. Many of the Government department campaigns are in this category, such as 'Don't Drink and Drive', 'Anti-smoking', and, more recently, the AIDS campaign. And, in the course of both selling and educating, quite a bit of information can be included (for example, in advertisements for films you're informed where and when they'll be shown).

But, although advertising is selling you something, it's not *exactly* selling, because then the people working in advertising would all be sales assistants, standing behind counters with the goods piled up in front of them. Advertising is selling you an *idea* about a product, a service, an organization, or a possible course of action. It is influencing you to buy Heinz baked beans when you go into a supermarket, to use British Rail's Supersaver next weekend, to vote for the Conservative party at the next election, or to limit your number of sexual partners to reduce the risk of catching AIDS. It is in its power to influence human behaviour that the fascination of advertising lies. And it *does* influence people: it's possible to prove this by sales figures and market research before and after advertising campaigns. For this reason, huge sums of money are spent on advertising and for this reason advertisers are bound by certain rules.

A Powerful Medium with Restrictions

Because advertising is so influential, advertisers have agreed to conform to certain rules, mainly laid down by themselves, and not by Parliament, except in the case of radio and television advertising, which are controlled by the 1981 Broadcast Act.

Television advertisements, thought to be the most powerful, are also the most restricted. For example, there is no cigarette advertising on television, although you will see advertisements for cigars and pipe tobacco. There is also an agreed code about alcohol: drinking mustn't be shown to give you an advantage romantically, and the people portrayed should not appear to be under 30. It's agreed that spirits won't be advertised on television, although wines (including vermouths), beers, port and sherry are allowed to be.

All scripts for television commercials, and the finished film, have to go to the IBA (Independent Broadcasting Authority) for approval. Printed advertisements come under the Advertising Standards Authority (ASA). People who want to complain about advertisements can write to the ASA, which examines all complaints on the basis of whether the advertisement has offended against the British Code of Advertising Practice. It regularly publishes case reports, giving the result of its investigations.

Advertisers, Agencies and the Media

People who work in advertising do not only work in agencies, as many people think. There are three sectors to advertising, as the diagram shows. None of these could flourish without the others. Take away the advertisers and the whole industry collapses. Take away the agencies and the expertise for producing the advertisements is lost. Remove the media and there is nowhere for the advertisements to appear.

The advertisers

You may have written an advertisement yourself – when you've been selling your car, flat or furniture, and have put them in the classified section of a newspaper. Say this cost you £50; you are an advertiser at the cheapest end of the market.

At the other end, there are organizations which spend a great deal on advertising (as much as £36,084,000 by British Telecom in 1986, for example). Who are the top spenders on advertising? The table on page 14 gives the top ten for 1986, grouped by industry.

This table illustrates some of the major types of advertisers. Other important areas are drink (alcohol), toiletries, cosmetics, pharmaceuticals (medicines), retail stores, financial, travel and fashion. Govern-

The Advertising Business

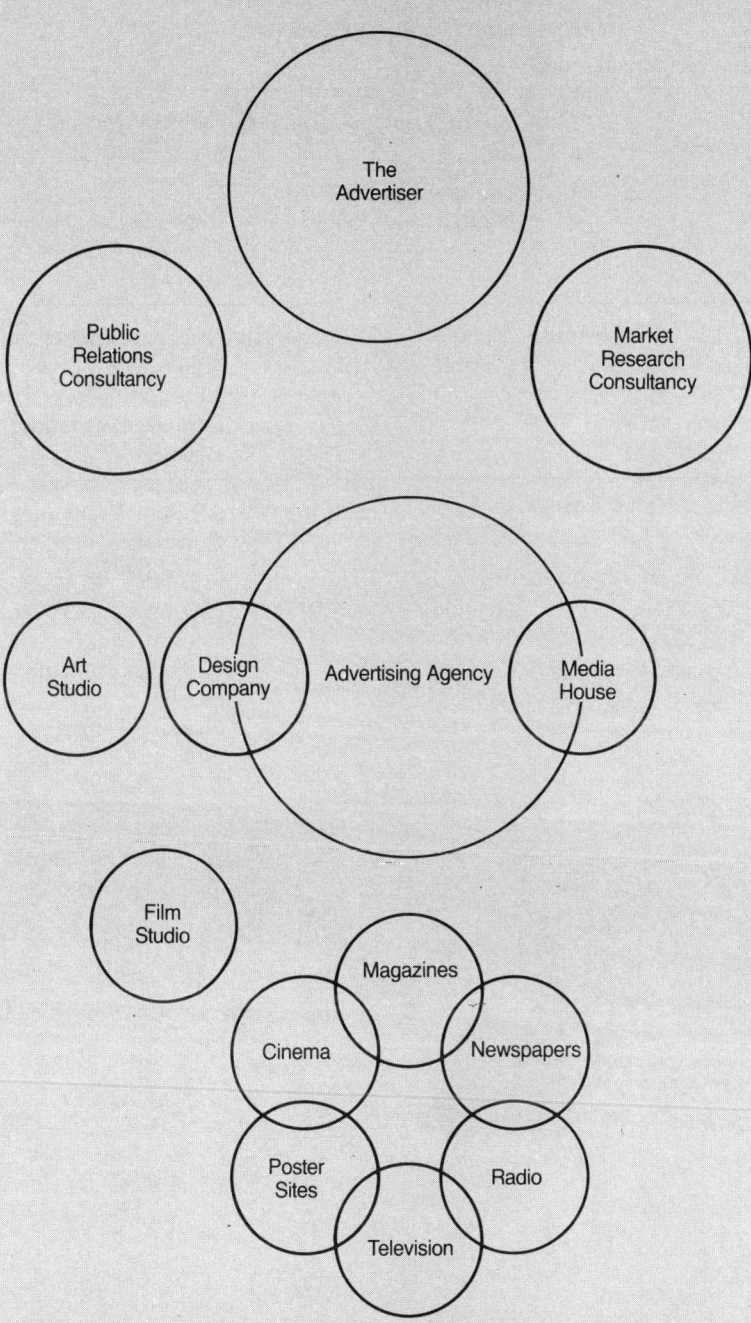

Table 1 TOP TEN SPENDERS ON ADVERTISING IN 1986.

INDUSTRY (in alphabetical order)	ADVERTISING	EXPENDITURE	PRODUCTS
Cars	Austin Rover	£27,737,000	Maestro, Metro, Mini, Montego, Rover
	Ford	£29,918,000	Capri, Escort, Fiesta, Granada, Orion, Sierra
Cleaning	Procter & Gamble	£35,263,000	Ariel Automatic, Bold 3, Daz Automatic, Fairy Liquid, Flash Liquid, Pampers
Food	Kellogg's	£29,451,000	All Bran, Branflakes, Cornflakes, Fruit 'n' Fibre, Special K
	Nestlé	£28,077,000	Crosse & Blackwell, Cook in Pot, Crosse & Blackwell Four Seasons Soup, Nescafé Coffee, Nescafé Gold Blend

Persil ads from
J. Walter Thompson

INDUSTRY (in alphabetical order)	ADVERTISING	EXPENDITURE	PRODUCTS
Fuel	British Gas	£26,571,000	Cookers, corporate energy, fires
	Electricity Council	£26,577,000	Cook Electric, corporate general, industrial storage
Government department	Department of Energy	£26,445,000	British Gas flotations, Energy Efficiency Office
Telecommunications	British Telecom	£36,084,000	Call stimulation, International Direct Dialling, Linkline, Yellow Pages
Tobacco	Imperial Tobacco	£27,344,000	Henri Winterman cigars, Imperial ESP cigars, Gold Block and St Bruno tobaccos, Lambert & Butler 100s, Players

ment departments are very important spenders on advertising. Put together, all the Government departments, including such diverse sections as the Data Protection Registrar and the Ordnance Survey, spent £81,350,000 in 1986.

Some of the advertisers in the table have been in the game a long time. J. Walter Thompson (JWT), an old established company and respected name in the business, opened its London office in 1899. One of its oldest clients is Kellogg's, which has been with JWT since 1938. Another long-established client is Persil.

Advertising is Part of Marketing

The advertising activity of the organizations in Table 1 is usually part of their marketing department. And it would not be a digression to stop to ask:

What is marketing?

People interested in advertising as a career are often also interested in marketing, and quite rightly so, as the two are closely linked. But what is the difference? When asked what marketing is, again, the reply is often that it's to do with selling, which is true. However, marketing is more than selling: it's deciding what will sell and to whom, getting it designed, manufactured, priced and packaged, promoting and advertising it, and *then* selling it. Marketing is, therefore, a wider concept than advertising or selling. This is something that has to be fully understood by the staff of an advertising agency, who may need to argue with the marketing department of a client that its marketing policy is at fault and that unless the name, price or distribution of the product is changed, the advertising campaign will be useless.

Marketing is a very important activity to any business venture. Products which are 'production led' (for example, *Today* newspaper, Concorde, the Sinclair C-5 car) are seldom huge commercial successes. To make something, no matter how technologically marvellous, and then hope that there are people out there who'll buy it, is an extremely risky business. It seldom works unless it's heavily subsidized. It's more sensible to find out if there is a market for a proposed product or even what the gaps are in an existing market and then produce products to fill them.

The agencies

What is an advertising agency? Why do advertisers use them? Why don't they employ their own copy-writers and designers, book their own insertions in the newspaper, and time on television?

Well, of course, a few do. Notably large stores who do the whole process themselves as they wish to react quickly to their stock and price situations. But almost every other company with a reasonable advertising budget will spend it via an agency. They do it in this way because they can buy the expertise and talent of people who would be unwilling to be employed simply on promoting one product. One argument sometimes used against advertising is that it employs very talented people in a very trivial business. Whether that is fair comment or not, the agencies certainly employ some very creative people – who, moreover, often move from agency to agency when they get tired of working with one group of clients.

The same argument applies to media buying: an agency is buying for a whole range of clients and therefore has more clout when getting the best prices from the media owners. The staff in this department build up expertise, which I suppose is the key reason for using an agency – its accumulated expertise.

There could also be another, more subtle, reason. Do the advertisers like using an agency because it somehow links them to a glamorous world separate from a bread-and-butter organization making tins of soup or selling railway journeys? Undoubtedly, the clients of the agency get wined and dined – sometimes flattered and cosseted – by the agency. The relationship could well have a deeper significance than the obvious business aspect.

The media

What is 'the media'? Careers officers turn pale when faced with someone who wants to work in 'the media'. Why? Because they know that, ten to one , this person doesn't know quite what the media is, or what they want to do. They are expressing other aspirations and views of themselves, saying they want to be Terry Wogan or Anna Ford. There's nothing wrong with this, and it could be interesting to discuss, but it belongs to an altogether wider sphere than careers advice.

The media are the means of communication, either by printed word (newspaper, magazines and posters) or by broadcasting (radio and television). Almost all newspapers and magazines depend, wholly or partly, on advertising to survive. The commercial television and radio stations do, too. Outdoor (poster) advertising sites, are mainly owned by specialist companies, whose business is to sell their panels to advertisers or their agents.

Advertising sales is a very distinct department on a publication or a television or radio station. Selling advertising is not a way into journalism or production: it is a career in its own right, with closer links to jobs in advertising agencies and advertisers than to the other jobs on a television station or publication.

Effective use of type and illustration, from Tango

LONDON SEEN PRESENTS

THE LAUNCH

parties on the river thames

WITH GUEST DJs PLAYING
LATIN · HOUSE · HIP-HOP · 70's
DISCO · FUNK · REGGAE · ETC

ASSEMBLE: WESTMINSTER PIER 7.45 pm
BOAT LEAVES: 8.00 pm PROMPT · RETURNS: 12.00 MIDNIGHT
TUBES: WESTMINSTER/EMBANKMENT

TICKETS: £6.00

THE PARTIES TAKE PLACE ON THE FOLLOWING DATES:

THURSDAY 23 JUNE
THURSDAY 14 JULY
THURSDAY 28 JULY
THURSDAY 11 AUGUST
THURSDAY 25 AUGUST

The specialist companies

Surrounding advertising agencies, like satellites, are a series of specialist companies. Sometimes people say they want to work in advertising, but, when questioned, what emerges is that they want to be actors in commercials or artists in studios. These are not jobs with an agency, for almost all the actual *production* of an advertisement is done outside the agency.

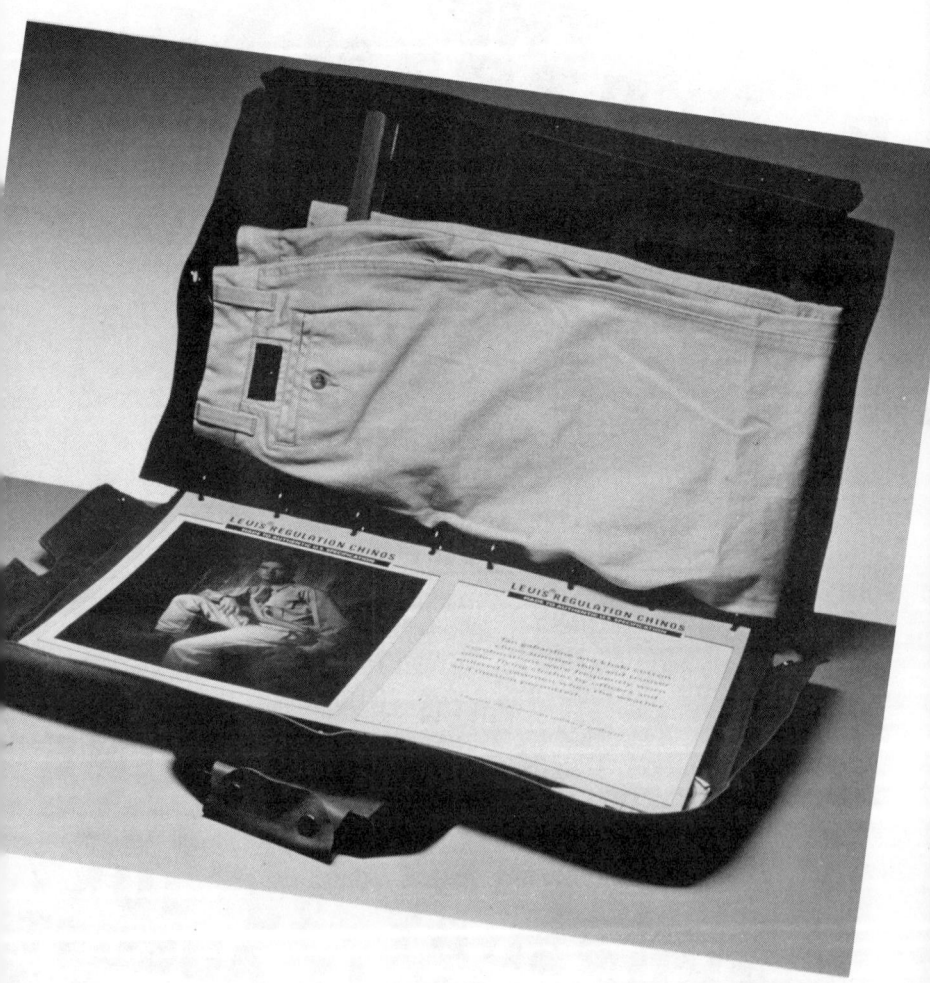

Advertising from
Baker Tamborini

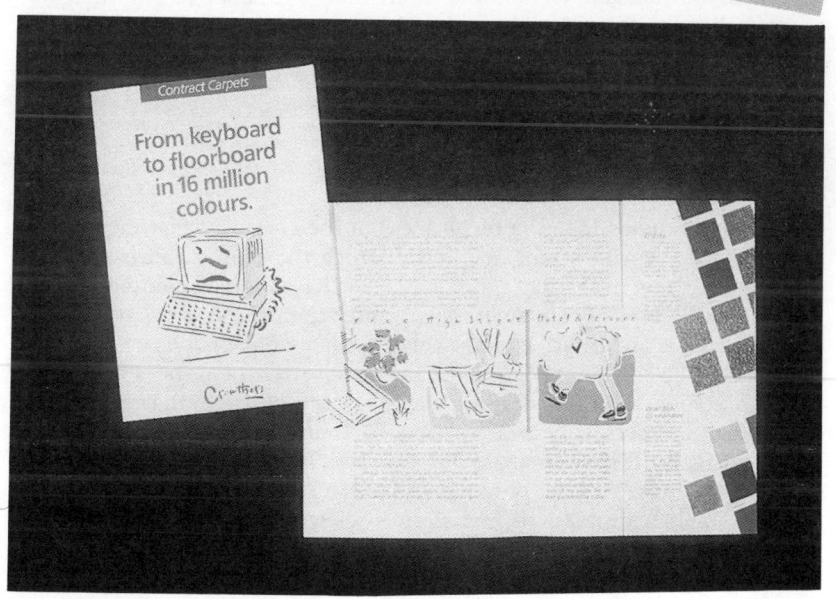

Film-production Companies

If a film is wanted for a television advertisement, the agency will commission an independent film-production company to make it. The actors are the same people who work on the stage or in feature films; this is not some separate acting career. Film-production companies have a nucleus of staff and employ all the others, such as directors, camera persons, actors and actresses, for a particular production.

Photographers and Illustrators

Similarly with photographers and illustrators (who are almost always freelance), and sometimes typographers. These will be commissioned according to the needs of the agency. Look at it this way. Highly creative people have a particular style. Every advertisement needs something different, so it would be counter-productive to keep, say, one photographer on the agency's staff. The art director will pick the photographer who does the sort of work required for, say, Benson & Hedges (Mick Dean or Bruce Brown).

Market Research

At the other end of the process, before the nature of the advertisement is decided upon, agencies may employ market-research companies to do research with them. The agency, along with the planning department, may need to work out what attitudes the public has to the way families or women are portrayed in advertisements, or what it thought about the previous campaign. Once this material has been collected, the agency can go ahead to develop ideas for the advertising campaign.

Art Studios

The art studios take the rough ideas of the creative department and produce them in a 'finished' form, which the printer can use. This involves a lot of accurate work which can have more in common with the skills of a draughtsman or a printer than those of what people think of as an 'artist'. It can involve a 'paste-up', which is, as it says, pasting up the component parts of the advertisement, on a board. It can involve some illustration (usually the technical or diagrammatic sort rather than very creative), photographic retouching, lettering or typography. These are jobs for a person who wants to carry out someone else's ideas, rather than have his or her own, and who is extremely neat, accurate and clean in their work.

Some agencies have their own studios, but more often they use one of the hundreds of independent art studios in existence.

Media Houses

The media houses (also known as media independents, agencies or shops) have the function of one department of an advertising agency – the media department. They advise advertisers on where to advertise, and buy space and time at the best price. They are valuable to the smaller agencies which have no media department and need to buy in this service. They are also sometimes used by advertisers who use several agencies and have decided to have all their buying done under one roof. Some clients avoid agencies altogether by using a media independent and a design consultancy.

The main difference, therefore, between working in a media independent and in the media department of an agency is that you are in direct contact with the client. There is no account executive, and the media staff are concerned with winning, keeping and communicating with the client themselves.

There are sometimes vacancies for A-level school-leavers in media independents, usually for numerate people with a grasp of business. Numerate graduates/HND people are also sometimes recruited.

The association of Media Independents (address on page 95) publishes a leaflet on the work of media independents, as well as a list of its members.

Design/Creative Consultancies

Design consultancies also offer the services of one of the departments of an agency – the creative department. The client who uses them, in conjunction with a media independent, can bypass an agency altogether.

If you are interested in any of these 'satellite' businesses, see some of the other books in this series.

Art studios, illustrators and design consultancies are covered more fully by *Getting Jobs in Graphic Design*. Film-production companies and photography will also have books of their own.

2
Working for an advertiser

To work in this sector of advertising really means going into marketing. Some companies may have a separate advertising department, or in a smaller company advertising may be part of publicity; but in most organizations, the people dealing with advertising will mainly be in the marketing department.

The advertising policy of a company will be decided in the context of its general marketing policy. Therefore, before deciding on what they aim to get from the next advertising campaign and how much to spend on it, the marketing department will be looking at sales figures, market research, reports from their sales force and direct customer reaction, in the form of complaints or compliments.

Choosing the services of an agency can be done at a very senior level in the company, sometimes by the managing director (as when Guinness left J. Walter Thompson for Allen Brady & Marsh), sometimes by the marketing director. Negotiation and liaison with the agency is very important, as is evaluation of the campaign. Did it succeed? Did the sales of the product rise by 20 per cent in April and May? Did the sales of their competitors fall? Have they increased their share of the market? Advertisers do not just want pretty advertising: they want results.

The advertiser can also be very fickle and change agencies for a variety of reasons. The account executive at the agency who got on so well with the advertiser may have left. The previous campaign may have failed. The advertiser may want to keep the agency on its toes and therefore review the situation every year.

The advertising staff in a company may also deal with other outside agencies, for example those organizing promotions, mailings, or devising a corporate image. In fact, they generally co-ordinate advertising for the marketing departments.

Many large companies run training schemes for graduates in marketing. Lists of these can be found in the various graduate directories (*Graduate Opportunities, Graduate Employment and Training*, and *Register of Graduate Employment and Training*) available in university and polytechnic careers advisory services. No particular degree subject is favoured, some ask for business studies or a technical subject, but mainly it is the person not the subject which is most important.

What should the person be like? Well, the employers are looking for someone with a sound business sense (the marketing department is very important to a company), who is good at communicating his or her point of view to colleagues and others, who has resilience and good organizational skills and, importantly, who is very numerate.

Everything in marketing is quantified. The success of an advertising campaign is quantified. A seat-of-the-pants reaction may be proved right, but the marketing manager wants to see the sales figures rise. This is reflected in the few jobs for school-leavers in this area. They are often in statistical work, producing information for the more senior people in the department.

The next section is about one particular advertiser: the Prudential. This company, like many in financial services, is rapidly expanding its marketing operation. It is not intended to be typical and the section should be read in conjunction with the general information.

Anatomy of an advertiser: the Prudential

The companies which have long-established marketing departments are those in 'FMCG' – or 'fast-moving consumer goods' to the uninitiated. However, in recent years, the marketing of financial services has begun to take off, and companies which were formerly ruled by actuaries are now beginning to look at their customers, at the services they require, and to promote what the company can offer.

142 Holborn Bars

One such company is the Prudential, at present in a stage of transition as far as marketing is concerned. In the early 1980s, marketing in the Prudential was spread over a number of departments. Now it is a recognized function and rapidly becoming a well-established one. However, its structure and policies are still being thrashed out.

You may have seen some of the Prudential's recent advertising – corporate advertising – which appeared around Christmas 1986. This was produced by their agency, Wight Collins Rutherford Scott. It starred Griff Rhys-Jones and was prepared in co-operation with the Group Public Affairs Department of the Prudential Corporation (the holding company), which is concerned with corporate identity, and which was responsible also for the new corporate identity of the Prudential, designed by Wolff Olins, who are still retained by the company.

Product advertising emanates from marketing departments within each of the Prudential group's divisions or subsidiary companies. In fact the specific department I visited, which is called Marketing Advertising and Promotion, is concerned with the products of Prudential Assurance, sold direct to the public through its own 12,000-strong direct sales force – the largest of its kind in Europe. This department employs 16 people and covers advertising and a number of related activities, such as direct mail, the production of leaflets, booklets and videos, promotional gifts, exhibitions and the necessary admin and accounts support.

Where the Staff Come From

Some of the staff have come from other departments of the Prudential. Miles Walters is one of them. He started off a few years ago on the Prudential's Youth Training Scheme (YTS), and now is one of the admin back-up. Likewise John Storm, who started at the Prudential's offices in Reading with O-levels and transferred to what was then the publicity department in the London head office about seven years ago. He has stayed in publicity/advertising/marketing ever since because this area interests him. He now works on customer promotions, of which more later.

Debbie Tyson, on the other hand, is a European business studies graduate who originally worked for an international trading company. She came to the Prudential just over a year ago when it took on five graduates. She now works on exhibitions.

Outside Suppliers

One characteristic of the department which all the staff liked was the contact with outside suppliers. The staff present the Prudential's views to outside people and assess their proposals for promotions, exhibitions, etc. The Prudential uses a series of specialists, usually the leaders in their field, which is why their advertising department is not bigger. On the whole, it doesn't design and print its own leaflets or stuff envelopes for its own mail shots – although it could if it had to, and does occasionally do so. So as well as Wolff Olins (corporate identity) which is retained by the Corporation, and WCRS Mathews Marcantonio (advertising agency) used by both the Corporation and some of its subsidiaries, the department also uses Broadwick Productions (to make creative sales/promotions/videos), Christian Brann (for its direct mail work), and various other designers, printers, production companies and distributors.

What the staff do

'Below The Line'

Many of the activities of the advertising department are 'below the line', which means the production of leaflets and booklets, promotional gifts and exhibitions, rather than the advertising the Prudential pays for in the media (i.e. above the line). To give you some idea of the diversity of work in the Prudential's advertising department, here is a brief description of what is done in the different sections.

Promotions

Promoting financial services is not easy because the promotion has to be appropriate to the product. For example, one scheme was tried where customers were offered free spending money for holidays overseas if they bought life-assurance policies. This was going off at such a tangent from life assurance that it didn't work. However, a scheme they are at present working on to launch their new domestic insurance policy tied this up with a home security service (Polycell Products) and seems likely to be a lot more successful. Buyers of Prudential's house insurance policies get a discount on the security products of Polycell. As there is such an obvious connection between domestic insurances and home security, this looks set to work. Also, a joint promotion like this keeps costs down and relates to the public perception of the Prudential. The success of a promotion depends on finding the right 'extra' for the service offered and the question is how many of the right 'extras' exist in the financial services field.

Exhibitions

Financial exhibitions are a real growth area. There were 3 in 1985 and 40 in 1988. Recently, the Prudential invested £30,000 in buying a stand and attended the Scottish Money Show, Debbie organized and co-ordinated this, deciding how to run the stand, how they'd deal with

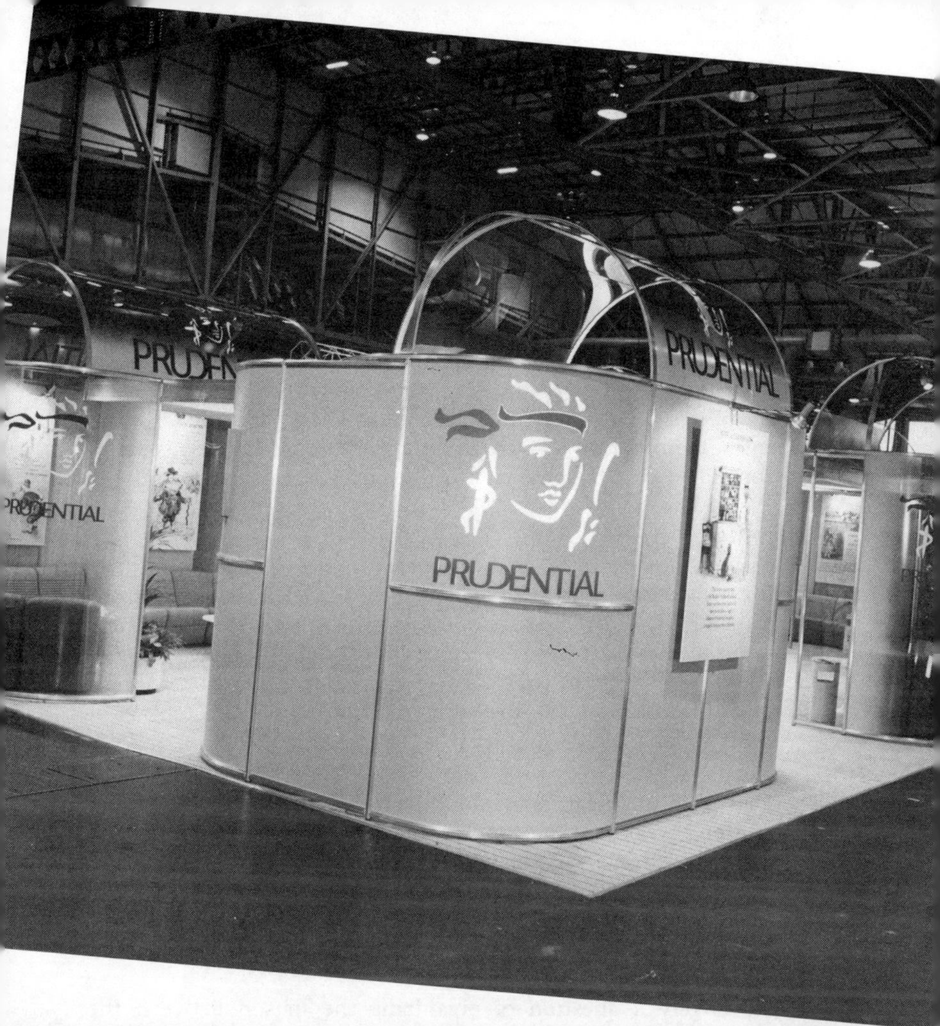
PRUDENTIAL
PRUDENTIAL
PRUDENTIAL
PRUDENTIAL

Money raised for expansion
PRU news
THE LAMP IN NEW HOMES
Districts join forces to win more business
down-to-earth message
NINE district managers' offices have joined forces to open up new business for the Prudential. Their ten-week sales campaign launched this month brings their own meaning to LAMP – the limited area marketing plans introduced this year.

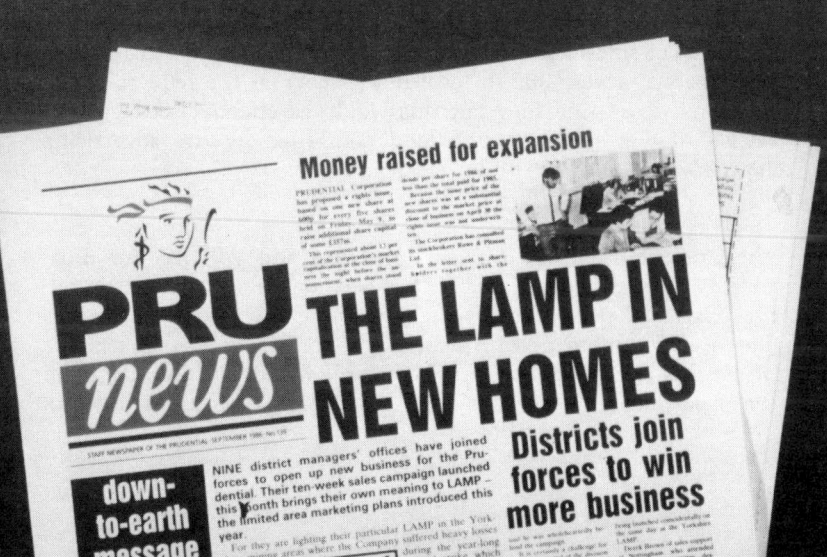

enquiries, follow them up, etc. Now the department is devising guide-lines and a training pack for the 12 divisional offices which will be attending some of the regional financial exhibitions springing up. Debbie and her colleagues plan to introduce the programme to the divisions at a training seminar held at head office.

Leaflets and Booklets

The department produce booklets, like the ones displayed on a literature rack or given to the sales force to use with their clients. These are designed by an outside company and approved by the Prudential Corporation so that the corporate identity is consistent. The copy is written by a member of the advertising department.

Direct Mail

The Prudential does a big mailing every year. With eight million existing policy-holders (1 in 5 households in the UK has a policy from the Pru) and lots of overseas customers, it has an excellent basis for mail shots. Each year it needs to let its ordinary branch policy-holders know their allocation of the year's profits, so it is able to add mail shots on different products, like unit trusts or pension quotations.

Videos

These are used as a means of communication for the company's direct sales staff based around the country and the indoor staff based at the company's head offices. When launching a new product to the staff, it is often cheaper to make a video than to go out to the 12 divisions regions and do a promotion.

Advertising

This is largely a question of organizing the liaison between the decision-makers at the Prudential and the agencies. The two people dealing with advertising cover Press, television, transport advertising (taxi and bus sides) and outdoor sites. Recently, there was a campaign for pensions, advertising in local newspapers (at the request of the divisions which said they felt this would be effective) designed by WCRS Mathews Marcantonio and controlled by the advertising department.

Training

The Prudential is very training-conscious and will pay for most courses the staff request. Debbie has been on a four-day, residential, financial marketing course which the company paid for. John has done the Communication Advertising Marketing (CAM) Certificate by evening classes at the City of London Polytechnic. Since being in the department, Debbie has done the Diploma of the Institute of

Marketing by distance learning. Miles did the Business Education Council (BEC) General while he was on the Youth Training Scheme (YTS).

Likes and Dislikes
They all liked the contact with outside agencies, and the fact they got out of the office about four or five days a month. They didn't like the lack of responsibility: in such a large corporation, every decision has to be referred upwards. One of them wondered whether it would be better to work in a smaller organization where this was not so much the case. They also disliked the fact that because the marketing department was still in the formative stages, they didn't always have enough to do.

Salary and Conditions
These were excellent; better than in the marketing department of an FMCG company, for example. Debbie thought a brand manager in such a company would be getting a third less for the same job. They thought it was a comfortable and stable existence.

There were two ways of seeing job prospects in the department: either as leading to a future within the Prudential – possibly in another department – or as a stepping-stone to a career outside in the advertising or marketing business.

3
Advertising agencies

Advertising agencies have a glamorous reputation and are frequently used as a setting for plays and novels. (Not that surprising: some copy-writers have become famous novelists, Dorothy L. Sayers and Fay Weldon, for example!). But most people will not have had first- or even second-hand experience of agencies unless they have friends or relations working there, or have been on work experience programmes.

The following quiz will show you how much you know. Add up your score when you get to the answers at the end of the chapter.

	True	False
1. There are lots of jobs in advertising.		
2. People in agencies are very arty and dress unconventionally.		
3. You don't need to be numerate in advertising.		
4. People in advertising agencies make commercials for TV.		
5. Only well-connected 'debby' types get into advertising.		
6. People in advertising work hard and long hours.		

How many jobs?

Advertising agencies sound like, and are, big business. In 1985 £4,441 million was spent on billing via advertising agencies. (Billings means the money spent on buying time and space in the media for advertising.)

Despite the huge sums of money, there are not huge numbers of agencies or huge numbers of staff. Three hundred agencies are members of the Institute of Practitioners in Advertising (IPA), which is the only accurate figure of their number available. There are other agencies, usually small, which do not belong to the IPA because they do not offer the full range of services. At a guess, there may be 800 agencies in all.

strategy for best tackling it. At this point, it is important that the account executive understands enough about marketing and the client's viewpoint to be able to discuss intelligently, and indeed argue about, what the client proposes. Is the name of the product wrong? Is the packaging likely to repel rather than attract? Having been through these stages, the account executive will write a marketing brief for the client, making recommendations about the advertising campaign. If the client accepts the marketing brief, it is time for the 'creative brief'. This goes to the creative department, which has to come up with the ideas.

There is no guarantee that the client will accept the most original and effective ideas. Indeed, the more original the idea, the more frightened the client may be. After all, the clients are usually business executives or Civil Servants who have to be convinced that the agency's fanciful ideas will be effective. Here the selling skills of the account executive come in. She (or he) must think of different ways of presenting the information until the client is convinced. At the same time, she must be able to keep the creative team happy. Above all, she must be able to judge whether the idea that the creatives have produced for the advertisement is commercially sound. It may be very funny or look beautiful, or use an entirely new technique, but will it sell tins of soup? Perhaps the client is right after all. These are the sorts of judgements the account executive has to make.

But suppose the client likes the idea, or one in a succession of ideas, what then? Does the account executive sit back and relax? Hardly. It is her responsibility to see that the advertisements are completed on time and appear where and when they are supposed to appear. If this doesn't happen, the client is not going to be happy. Furthermore, the client is not going to pay. The account executive's role involves continued liaison with the creative department (which has chosen the film director/illustrator/photographer it wants), with the production department, which is organizing the schedules for all this to happen (which now become very important to the account executive), and with the media department, which is buying the space and time.

When the campaign is over, it is time to review its success. The client's sales department will be quick to tell the agency whether the target has been met and whether the firm has increased its percentage of the baked bean market by 10 per cent or not. The client may have been getting fan mail for the advertising, or a lot of letters signed 'Disgusted of Tunbridge Wells'! All these have to be taken into account. However, if the client is satisfied and does not make an annual review of which agency to use, the account executive will move on with the client to the next campaign, and the next.

Account executives often say they spend most of their time in meetings. These can be meetings out of the office, perhaps involving catching a plane one day a week to the other end of the country to

An Advertising Agency

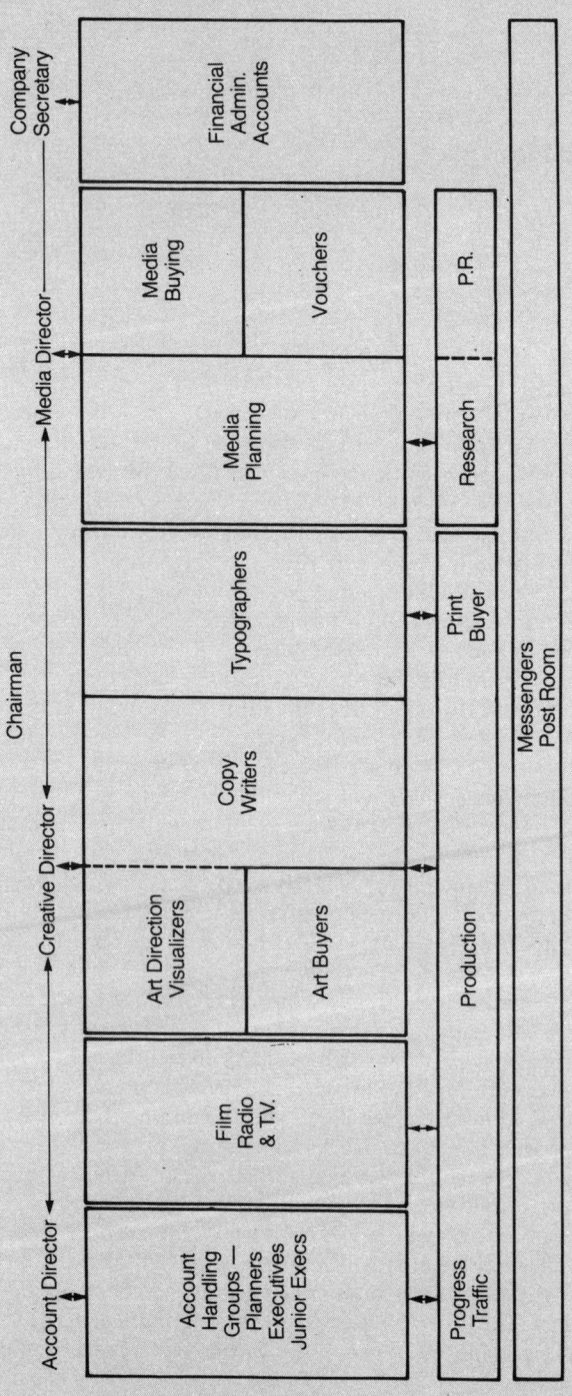

Chairman

Account Director

Creative Director

Media Director

Company Secretary

Account Handling Groups — Planners Executives Junior Execs

Film Radio & T.V.

Art Direction Visualizers

Art Buyers

Copy Writers

Typographers

Media Planning

Media Buying

Vouchers

Financial Admin. Accounts

Research

P.R.

Progress Traffic

Production

Print Buyer

Messengers Post Room

visit a client, or meetings with the account group of each client within the agency. When they're not in meetings, they are often writing reports and letters and reading material relevant to the client and the campaign.

So what makes a good account executive? Well, it's important to have an outgoing, attractive and persistent personality. Different clients will suit different account executives, so there is some room for a variety of personalities, providing they all have good 'people' skills. They also need a sound business sense: this is not a job for the commercially naïve dilettante. Account executives must be enthusiasts and able to cope with a lot of pressure, including, on occasion, long hours.

In the large agencies, graduate trainees are recruited to be account executives. In a small or medium-sized agency, a junior who has started in some other department, such as production, could be promoted to account executive.

The Account Planner

This not a job found in every agency, although it has been developed extensively in some of the leading ones, such as Boase Massimi Pollitt and J. Walter Thompson.

The account planner's job is really a cross between the 'marketing–thinking' part of the account executive's job and that of a qualitative market researcher. (*Qualitative* market research is talking in depth to a few consumers about their feelings and the motivation behind their behaviour, rather than the more traditional *quantitative* market research, which is gathering facts and figures.) The account planner is really a representative of the consumer, finding out about and understanding the customer's attitude to the product and to the advertising. The planner may commission research (usually quantitative) or carry out his or her own research (qualitative). All this is very important for developing both the marketing and creative strategies, and the planner will often present the creative ideas to groups of consumers as the ideas are developed.

Although the planner is like the account executive, in needing a good business sense and good communication skills, he or she can be a more academic type than the account executive – especially able at looking at material and drawing conclusions.

Some agencies take graduate trainees into account planning, whereas others recruit people who already have experience in marketing, market research or some other area of advertising.

The Creative Department

The single most important department in the agency, the one on which the agency stands or falls, is the creative department which produces the ideas for campaigns, both the words (copy) and the visuals. There are a number of different jobs in a large creative department, starting with the boss, the creative director. The **creative director** could have started as an art director, but more usually has been a copy-writer, 'because the copy-writer has the mouth'. (Not all copy-writers are 'barrow-boy' types; there is quite a variety and some are scholarly or Civil Servantish.)

The creative director is presented with the ideas by his pairs of art directors and copy-writers; he or she decides which ones are good enough to pass on to the client.

The **art directors** have almost always taken an advertising-biased graphic design course (see Chapter 8). Their job is to come up with the visual ideas for the advertisement and it can become almost a managerial function when it comes to an advertisement's production, choosing (often – but there may be an art buyer) the art studio, certainly the film director, photographer, etc.

At one time, the copy-writer and the art director worked separately. The copy-writer worked out the idea and the words, and sent it over to the art director, who designed it. Now the two work on the campaign together from the beginning and the art director can write and the copy-writer draw if they have the ability and are so inclined. Draughtsmanship is not that important to the art director; other experts can carry out his or her ideas. The rough idea is presented to the client in the form of a drawing or sketch in the case of printed matter, or a story-board (pictures of crucial points in the narrative) in the case of a film. Only when the client likes it all does it go into production.

Of course, we know that the client may not like it: he may make petty criticisms, saying that the walls of the room portrayed in the advertisement should be green not blue, because green is his wife's favourite colour, and the creative team must grin and bear it. And the creativity is not always that creative. Severe limitations are imposed not only by the agreed restrictions on some advertisements, but by what is being advertised and by the fact that at the end of the day the advertisement has to sell the product. So, whereas a campaign highlighting the problems of nurses in the National Health Service may raise a hundred and one good and interesting points, a campaign for a new lager is likely to make him feel, as one copy-writer said, 'sick in the stomach'. For what can be said about lager that has not already been said in a hundred other campaigns? What one point can be found that will sell the stuff? Then there is the vast mass of more technical, printed advertising. At least the lager campaign is likely to have a big budget and advertisements on the telly, whereas garden sheds and bulldozers will not.

The speciality of many **copy-writers** is explaining the technical to the layman, without getting too boring. The copy-writer (sometimes known simply as a writer) has a skill different from the journalist or the novelist. The copy is often restricted to very few words (some television advertisements have none at all: the name is *seen* in a 'pack shot' of the product rather than heard), and every word has to tell. Very often the words are of the street, spoken English rather than literary English, and, of course, in broadcast advertising they are spoken. So the copy-writer must be in touch with current thinking, social trends and their expression. You will have seen a lot of advertisements recently with assertive women and losing men. This is not because advertising agencies are out to change society, but because they are out to please the viewers. There are also a lot of situation comedies on television with the same relationship portrayed. The viewers like to see themselves in a certain light: this is how they are, how they think they are, or how they think they would like to be.

How do you become a copy-writer? There is no one way. There are two specialist copy-writing courses at Watford and Hounslow Colleges (see Chapter 8). Some copy-writers have started in a junior position in the agency, had their writing noticed or brought it to the attention of the creative department, and got in that way. Others have started in some other career, which could be almost anything (sales, teaching, the Civil Service), and got together a portfolio or asked to take an agency's copy test. At one time it was possible for the aspiring copy-writer to be accepted on the strength of a good copy test. Now this is much less likely and most agencies expect to see examples of a copy-writer's work, as they do of an art director's, especially as copy-writers and art directors so often work in pairs now and produce a joint portfolio. If you are an aspiring copy-writer working in another occupation, you score if you have kept up your own writing, studied and copied the style of successful advertisements, and have put together a portfolio of your work. Here, of course, those who have attended the courses have an advantage. They have prepared portfolios over one or two years and have something substantial to show.

Besides copy-writers and art directors, is there anyone else in the creative department? The biggest agencies will have art buyers and typographers. The **art buyer** takes over some of the work which would be done by the art director in a smaller agency. This involves choosing the art studio, ordering the artwork and buying in other services, such as printers for posters, bus sides, etc.

Overleaf: Magazine ad from Bartle, Bogle & Hegarty

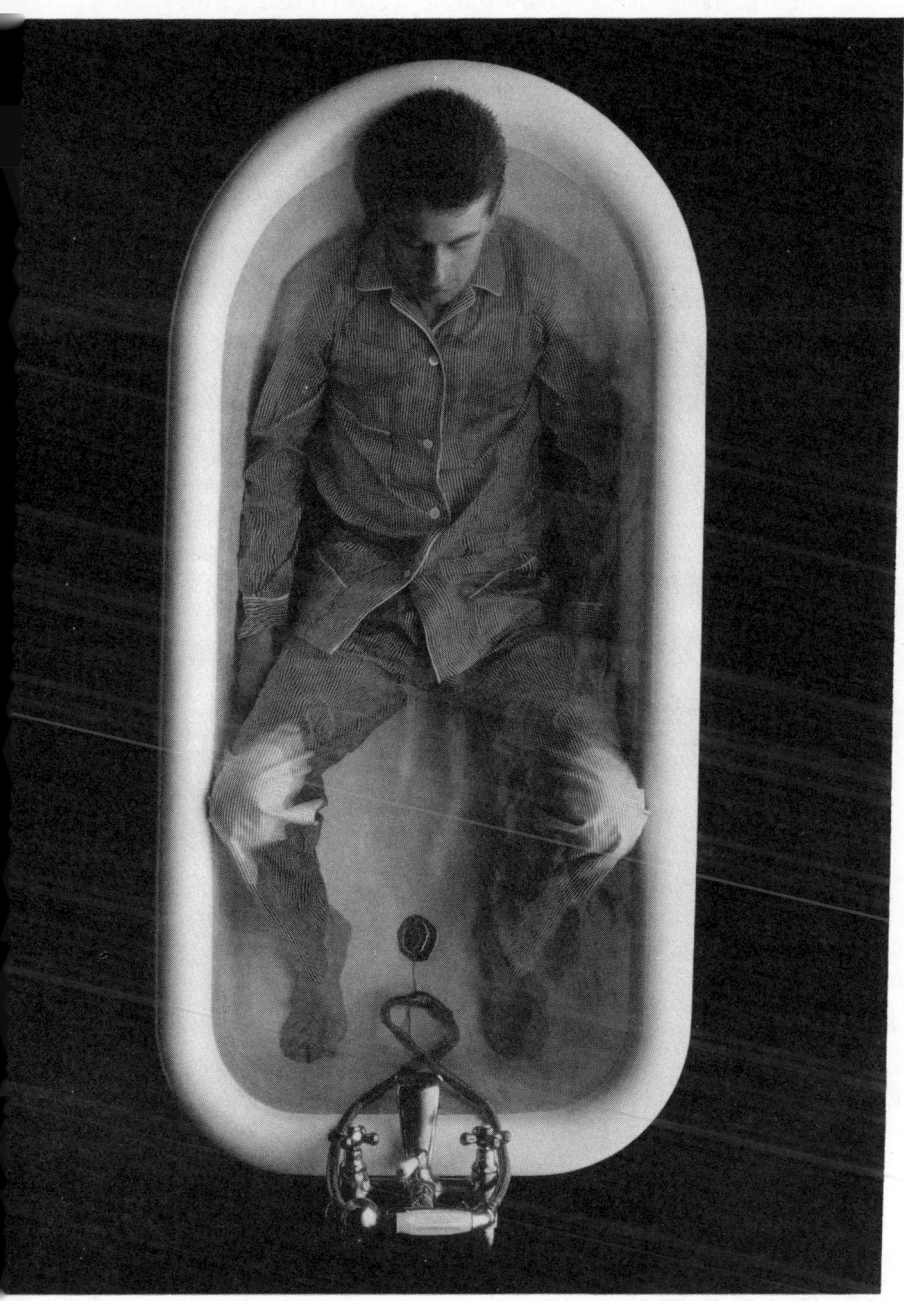

The **typographer** is a specialist sort of designer, usually with an art college qualification. His or her own speciality is the appearance of printed matter, choosing from hundreds of typefaces and instructing the typesetting house. Typographers also work in art studios.

Cascade® Script 12 **117** (21)

defghijklmnopqrstuvwxyz
CDEFGHIJKLMNOPQRSTUVWXYZ
34567890 .,;:"«»&!?

ambûrgefönstiv iam admodum mitiq

Caslon Antique roman/normal/romain 12 **110** (21)

defghijklmnopqrstuvwxyz
CDEFGHIJKLMNOPQRSTUVWXYZ
4567890 .,;:"«»&!?

bûrgefönstiv iam admodum mitigati raptarum animi erant sed earum parente
maxime sordida veste lacrimisque et querelis civitates concitabant undique l

Caslon Antique italic/kursiv/italique 12 **108** (21)

defghijklmnopqrstuvwxyz
CDEFGHIJKLMNOPQRSTUVWXYZ
4567890 .,;:"«»&!?

bûrgefönstiv iam admodum mitigati raptarum animi erant sed earum parentes
maxime sordida veste lacrimisque et querelis civitates concitabant undique lega

Caslon Old Face 2 roman/normal/romain 8/12* **111/116** (21)

defghijklmnopqrstuvwxyz
CDEFGHIJKLMNOPQRSTUVWXYZ
34567890 1234567890 .,;:"«»&!?

bûrgefönstiv iam admodum MITIGATI RAPTARUM ANIMI erant sed earum
tes tum maxime sordida veste lacrimisque et querelis civitates concitabante

Caslon Old Face 2 italic/kursiv/italique 8/12* **103/105** (21)

defghijklmnopqrstuvwxyz
CDEFGHIJKLMNOPQRSTUVWXYZ
34567890 1234567890 .,;:"«»&!?

bûrgefönstiv iam admodum mitigati raptarum animi erant sed earum parentes tu
ne sordida veste lacrimisque et querelis civitates concitabant undique legatione mi

Caslon Old Face heavy/fett/gras 18 **130** (16)

cdefghijklmnopqrstuvwxyz
BCDEFGHIJKLMNOPQRSTUVW
Z 1234567890 .,;:"«»&!?

åmbûrgefönstiv iam admodum ni

Caslon 3 roman/normal/romain 8/12* **131/136** (21)

cdefghijklmnopqrstuvwxyz
BCDEFGHIJKLMNOPQRSTUV
XYZ 1234567890 1234567890 .,;:"«»
nbûrgefönstiv iam admodum MITIGATI RAPTARUM ANIMI eran
earum parentes tum maxime sordida veste lacrimisque et quer

13046 Caslon 3 italic/kursiv/italique 8/12* **124/126** (21)

abcdefghijklmnopqrstuvwxyz
ABCDEFGHIJKLMNOPQRSTUV
XYZ 1234567890 .,;:"«»&!?

Håmbûrgefönstiv iam admodum mitigati raptarum animi eran
um parentes tum maxime sordida veste lacrimisque et querelis

05047 Caslon 540 roman/normal/romain 12 **125** (21)

abcdefghijklmnopqrstuvwxyz
ABCDEFGHIJKLMNOPQRSTUV
XYZ 1234567890 1234567890 .,;:'«»&

Håmbûrgefönstiv iam admodum MITIGATI RAPTARUM ANIMI era
um parentes tum maxime sordida veste lacrimisque et querelis

13047 Caslon 540 italic/kursiv/italique 12 **110** (21)

abcdefghijklmnopqrstuvwxyz
ABCDEFGHIJKLMNOPQRSTUVWX
1234567890 .,;:'«»&!?

Håmbûrgefönstiv iam admodum mitigati raptarum animi erant sed e
ntes tum maxime sordida veste lacrimisque et querelis civitates concita

09364 Caslon black/fett/gras 18 **137** (26)

abcdefghijklmnopqrstuvwxyz
ABCDEFGHIJKLMNOPQRSTUVW
1234567890 .,;:"«»&!?

Håmbûrgefönstiv iam admo

42049 Caslon open face/licht/éclairé 12 **113** (21)

abcdefghijklmnopqrstuvwxyz
ABCDEFGHIJKLMNOPQRSTU
XYZ 1234567890 .,;:"«»&!?

Håmbûrgefönstiv iam admodum n

03552 Caslon ITC® No. 224 book/Buch/texte 12 **129** (06)

abcdefghijklmnopqrstuvwxyz
ABCDEFGHIJKLMNOPQRSTUVX
1234567890 .,;:"«»&!?

Håmbûrgefönstiv iam admodum mitigati raptarum animi er
rum parentes tum maxime sordida veste lacrimisque et que

54552 Caslon ITC® No. 224 book italic/Buch kursiv/texte italique 12 **135** (06)

abcdefghijklmnopqrstuvwxyz
ABCDEFGHIJKLMNOPQRSTUVWZ
1234567890 .,;:"«»&!?

Håmbûrgefönstiv iam admodum mitigati raptarum animi
earum parentes tum maxime sordida veste lacrimisque et

The Media Department

This department's responsibility is to make sure that the advertisement reaches the right target group at the lowest possible media cost.

Advising on how best to reach the 'right target group' is the job of the **media planner**, who may be in on the discussions with the client or receive the brief from the account executives. The planner will have access to all the complex data on who watches what, reads what and listens to what, produced by JICNARS (Joint Industry Committee for National Readership Surveys), BARB (Broadcasters' Audience Research Board), the agency's own research, and by various other independent surveys.

The client will have in mind a certain group he wishes to sell to – by age, sex, income, occupation and geographical area. The job of the account planner is to advise on what is the best way to reach this group.

Planners need to be very numerate and are often graduates. As well as the usual agency requirements of being able to communicate and work well in a team, the planner needs to be able to identify the most relevant information out of the mass of facts available and translate this into the best solution for the problem.

The **media buyers** have to reach the right target group at the *lowest possible media cost*. The buyers will be passed a detailed brief by the planners and will then go ahead to book the space in publications and the time on the air (on radio and television) at the best price they can get. It is normal to specialize, especially in a big agency, in either television or print buying, or even in outside poster sites or periodicals.

Buying space and time is more complex than it sounds. Television-time buying especially is a high-pressure business, operating a bit like a commodity market. Although there are set rates for the time, these can vary either up or down according to the demand for a particular spot. Media buyers are acute commercial types, who could operate well in some of the City dealing careers. The same skills are required: a feel for the market-place and the market price, the ability to cope with people who are professional sellers, and being numerate, accurate and articulate.

Media is one of the departments which is not so graduate dominated. There are vacancies for school-leavers, often A-level age and standard, and sometimes for younger people.

The Production Department

The production department deserves to be described as a specialist advertising department, although it does not have the 'status' of account handling or creative or media, probably because it does a lot of the hard work!

This department is responsible for seeing that the advertisements are produced in the right form to a high enough standard approved by all the correct people, and dispatched to the right place by the deadline. Its staff are constantly in touch with the other departments of the agency.

In a large agency, the responsibility for the progress of an advertisement is separated from the responsibility for its production. There is another department, called traffic or control or progress, to cover the first function.

The production department has to be knowledgeable about the different methods of printing used by various newspapers and magazines and to provide the advertisement in the right form to be printed by letterpress, litho or gravure. The advertisement must also be produced to the right size to fit the publication. The production department gives details of the size of advertisement required to the creative department, who will pass this on to whichever art studio it commissions. The printed words will be commissioned from a typesetting house, after discussions about the size and style of type between the typographer (either from the agency or the art studio) and the art director. The type is sent, with the layout, to the studio, where it is pasted up and returned to the production department to get the approval of everyone concerned (the art director, the copy-writer, the typographer): not an easy task, as time is often short and the artwork may have to be put on the train 'Red Star' to where the paper is printed.

A similar process takes place in television production. The agency will commission a film company to make the commercial. In large agencies there will be a separate television production department with producers responsible for the film being made and its cost, just as a producer making a feature film for the cinema or television will have these responsibilities. The directors, the actors, the camera team and everyone else will be employed by the film-production company. Making a film is a very costly business, and in this type of production it is important to have very strict estimating procedures, as well as the usual timing plan.

Once the film company has shot the commercial, it is edited. The film goes through a 'double head' stage, at which the sound-track and the visuals are on separate pieces of track. The film may be shown to the client at this stage. Then the final copies are made and distributed. The ITA (Independent Television Authority) has to approve both the script and the finished film, before it can be broadcast. The advertising agency may also submit the script to its own lawyers.

Production is a good department for school-leavers to get started in, or, in a larger agency, for an HND person to begin. Working in the production department is a good way of learning about all the departments of the agency, as production is in touch with them all. The staff of the production department have to be both tactful and persistent as they have no power to make the creative department hurry. They must, of course, be very well organized and accurate.

Television producers come in to their jobs from a variety of routes. Some have been in another job in advertising; others may have come from a film-production company; yet others have started as secretaries or personal assistants to producers and learned so much they have become producers in their own right.

What qualities are required?

As I've gone along I've outlined the personal qualities required in the different jobs in an agency. As you can see, there are a variety of jobs requiring a variety of different talents, skills and qualities. Is it possible to make any generalizations about the people most likely to get in to advertising?

One very important factor is the genuine desire to get in and succeed. This will show itself as 'keenness' and 'enthusiasm' and 'willingness' (being willing often means being willing to make the tea and buy the sandwiches). People in advertising are friendly, with attractive outgoing personalities, well dressed and good communicators. They are persistent (this shows itself by the fact they got there in the first place) and resilient to disappointment: the client may keep on turning down the creative department's ideas; the pitch for the new account which kept you at work all weekend may fail! they are interested in advertisements and are willing to subordinate extreme individuality to team-work.

Answers to quiz

1. There are lots of jobs in advertising? False. (See How many jobs and Where are the jobs sections.)

2. People in agencies are very arty and dress unconventionally? False. Almost everyone in an agency is smartly and fashionably dressed. The creative department may dress more casually, but they are usually smart and fashionable too.

3. You don't need to be numerate? Mainly false. Numeracy is very important, particularly in some jobs – media, production. It's not vital for, say, copy-writers or art directors.

4. People in advertising agencies make commercials for TV? False. The films are made by film-production companies commissioned by the agency. (See Chapter 1.)

5. Only well-connected 'debby' types get into advertising? False. There are all types in advertising – the street-wise Eastenders as well as the public school boy or girl.

6. People in advertising work hard and long hours? True! Numbers employed in agencies have *dropped* since the 1960s, while the money spent on billings has increased. Agencies do not carry passengers and have to meet deadlines – even if this means working evenings and weekends.

If you got all 6 right you probably already work in advertising or you've already read the rest of this book! If you've only got 1 or 2 right, then you need to read the rest of this book! If 3 to 5, then you are well informed in some areas; now find out more.

4

Anatomy of an agency: Bartle Bogle Hegarty, or how to get it right

Bartle Bogle Hegarty (BBH) is a young agency and has around 140 staff. It had eight founding partners and has grown rapidly to its present size. It has offices in Great Pulteney Street which are elegant, purposeful and very modern.

All advertising agencies have their own character, and this one came across to me as having a tremendous dedication to creativity and professionalism, a very civilized place where the staff enjoyed working.

The staff I met, from six different departments, were full of advice for would-be entrants to advertising and details about the agency and their jobs.

Account Handler

Chris Abel was dedicated to getting into advertising and into BBH. He decided on advertising two years before he left university, which gave him time to find out about the business and the individual agencies. He ordered *Campaign* and consulted a book called *Portfolio*, which lists what agencies have what accounts, shows pictures of the ads, and tells you what the agency's philosophy is. He applied to all major agencies (30 to 50 applications) and had six interviews (second interviews with two), and in the end got a job in a small agency (Mallett McCormick, with 40 staff) as a trainee account handler. You get responsibility sooner in a small agency and after two to three months Chris was presenting to clients. After a year, he was approached by a 'head hunter'. He told her the only agency he was interested in was BBH, and got taken on by them.

Chris said the agency had a definite character, which is based on protecting the advertising. It assumed that you can do the admin part of the job; what is more important is that you are expected to think and add to the creative process. For this reason, the agency has very strict systems, designed to give a lead time of six weeks to the creatives. This means that a client could expect to wait two or three months before he saw any advertising. There were various maxims around this: 'Don't take the first idea – take the best idea', and 'The ad you think you won't be able to sell (i.e. to the client) could well be a great idea'.

There are stacks of reasons for flying Piedmont to Charlotte. This isn't one of them.

aily Gatwick flight to North Carolina is the sole international arrival at Charlotte. So it's not surprising that in one hour you're through to catch one of 358 daily departures to 76 US cities.

PIEDMONT

Successful advertisements from Bartle Bogle Hegarty for Piedmont Airlines (above) and frames from the TV ad for Audi.

Vorsprung durch Technik.

There were also some maxims for the wise account handler: 'Trust no-one and expect nothing to happen', 'If it goes wrong, assume it's your fault'. A lot of account handling is orchestrating events and making sure things do happen. Also, particularly in this agency, there is emphasis on protecting the creatives from undue stress.

Chris works long hours (usually 8.30 – 7.00), and says that if you're work shy, don't go into advertising. Because of the hours it can also be the end of your social life. He also said that once people join BBH, very few leave, 'because it's a good and fun place to work' with a lot of the best advertising people in London. Indeed, the agency was set up with the idea of having fun, and as Chris said, 'as it's hard work, if you don't enjoy it what's the point?'

Is there a lot of entertaining of clients if you're an account handler? Another BBH maxim: 'Good advertising – not long lunches'. Certainly clients were entertained (they have a Christmas party and a Boulogne outing for one of his clients), but this agency didn't rely on entertaining. There are some agencies where the account handlers have built up their reputation on lunching clients – but not here! Certainly the client should look forward to coming to the agency. He or she should feel confident about the agency and will then be more likely to be in a relaxed frame of mind and buy the advertising.

BBH have a policy of 'growing their own' and Chris envisages staying with them for the foreseeable future.

Media Planner/Buyer

Debbie Boyes defined the media department for me: 'The media department is a group of people who pass as experts on the basis of their prolific ability to produce an infinite variety of incomprehensible statistics calculated with micrometric precisions from vague assumptions based on debatable evidence from inconclusive data derived by companies of doubtful reliability for the sole purpose of misleading an already confused group of persons who never look at numbers anyway'!

Debbie originally planned to be an accountant (and even had a place at the London School of Economics to study it) but decided to do a secretarial course instead. Then she got a job as a secretary in a merchant bank, moving on to selling a 'traded currency fund' (a basket of currencies) to both institutional and private investors. But she decided that advertising would be more in line with her temperament. She decided to do the Communication Advertising and Marketing (CAM) course (3 nights a week, 3 hours a night), at the College for the Distributive Trades in London. She got a media job with Cogent Elliott (after originally applying for account handling because she'd never heard of media), 'By refusing to take no for an answer'. Two years later she moved to BBH.

What makes a good media person? Debbie thought the right personality and the ability to negotiate the best value were very important. 'You must be able to pick up on what the advertising sales people are like and get the best out of them. You have to be one step ahead.'

Is ability with figures important? 'You do have to be able to think figures, although it's more basic arithmetic than A-level maths.'

The planning part of Debbie's job took up more time than the buying. Planning could take two months, whereas the buying could take two days or a week, depending on what media were being used. The media planning comes in early in the process of planning the advertising campaign. The media department looks at the creative department's brief, gets the media brief for itself and 'keeps on talking to the others'. In fact, like the account handlers, the media department was encouraged to mix a lot with the creative department and contribute to the creative process.

Debbie would consult various reference materials (like the 'National Readership Survey' and the 'Target Group Index') before recommending in which publications etc. the advertising should appear to reach the target audience. She also has to consider the timing – for example, one of the clients, Dr White's Sanpro, would have all year round advertising, whereas another client, Piedmont Airlines, may want its advertising particularly strong in January when historically sales are not so good for airlines.

Debbie wouldn't want to be in account handling now; she feels they are under too much pressure from both the clients and the creatives. The BBH media department has only been in existence a short time; before it was set up, BBH used media independents. They never assumed that the agency's clients would automatically use them and so they had to sell their service to the clients.

Copy-writer

Will Awdry worked as an account man for two years, resigned and put together a portfolio with an art director he had met, and got a job at the first place he brought his portfolio to – BBH. He reckons that he and his partner were very lucky, as every day several portfolios are brought into the agency for John Hegarty to have a look at.

There are several advantages to working in the creative department of this particular agency (as you will have gathered from the account handler's and media buyer/planner's stories). One is, as Will put it, that they 'soften up' the client by telling him what he ought to expect in the way of creative work. The result of this is that the client is usually pleased to see the advertising and things rarely get thrown out. This avoids the frustration that creatives can experience in other agencies. The other good thing is that they don't do creative pitches. This means that the account handler will do a presentation to a potential client, and the planner will analyse what the problem is, but the creative work won't start until the client is won. This means no Government departments use BBH, as they insist on creative pitches.

Does a copy-writer sit and write all day? Not exactly. Sometimes Will does sit with a pad of paper, scribbling and talking to his art director partner to see if anything comes. He finds his attention span for this is about 40 minutes; after this he has to leave it, do something else and then come back. Will also goes to meetings, presents his ideas to John Hegarty, looks at students' books, sees photographers, illustrators, etc. and commissions them. He has to check ads throughout and sign to say they're right.

Is it easy to find ideas for ads? 'There are times when you wake up at three in the morning screaming because you can't think of a line for yoghurt.' A lot of ideas are discarded before the final advertisement. For the Latex advertisement, Will and partner came up with enough ideas to wallpaper a room in ads. Within two weeks they showed 30 to John Hegarty, who chose three. These grew into another 40, and six of them were presented to the client, who wanted to do four of them.

Who does what between the copy-writer and the art director? 'You're there to bolster each other up, and after a bit it becomes seamless. You forget which one of you came up with the idea.'

Will is also involved in the production side, going to shoots for television commercials and playing director for radio commercials. For all this, you need a tactful streak. There are some copy-writers who get by, by being bloody-minded prima-donnas but you're dealing with a lot of people every day and this doesn't necessarily work. There are 16 in the film crew, and when you have to say what you think is wrong when its three in the morning, over the head of the director, while the set is beginning to wilt and you're going into triple overtime, tact can very useful if you don't want bloodshed. For commercials, Will and the team choose the director and are there at the casting sessions. He attended a leg casting for Pretty Polly tights!

Will thought BBH was civilized (there weren't many raised voices), perhaps too civilized. 'The path to mediocrity is paved with good decisions.' I'm not sure if that's a maxim!

Do copy-writers ever run out of ideas? It varies. Some people get better, some trail off, some reach a pinnacle and stay there. It's possible to be terrified that your ideas will trail off and this paranoia hastens the copy-writer's demise. Some creatives, like John Hegarty, just love advertisements, and they are perhaps the most successful.

Accounts Department

Denise Webber was working in the accounts department
of a courier firm. Her sister worked in advertising and Denise met
people from advertising and liked them. She went to an employment
agency who found her a job with BBH.

The accounts department has various sections: bought ledger,
cashiers, petty cash and expenses, and management accounting. They
also do the accounts for two subsidiary companies: Tango (a design
company) and Limbo (below the line advertising).

Denise finds her job everything she expected it to be. She wanted to
work with people of a similar age and interest, and finds an advertising agency is more fun to work for than her previous company. In this
agency, the accounts department is thought of as an integral part of
the company. In others, this may not be so.

Denise wants to stay in accounts, although at one point she was
considering moving to production. On the whole, the accounts staff
do tend to stay in accounts. However, one person left, came back and
got a job as a PA in the television department.

Denise works on management accounting, interpreting the figures
gathered by the accounts department. She also produces any special
information required – such as, how much money do we spend on
travel? – and sorts out queries about artists' payments (mainly the
repeat fees paid to actors when their commercial is shown again).

She is studying in her own time and has passed accounting A-level

53

and is now taking economics. When she has the two A-levels, she may choose to study for a qualification in certified accountancy (although this will be three evenings a week for four years).

Her official hours of work are 9.15 – 5.30, but the main thing is that you get your work done and make a good contribution. She usually works 9.30 to 6.00, 6.30 or 7.00. Everyone works hard and this is appreciated, so if someone wants to take a longer lunch to meet a special friend, that's OK, because people know you'll make up the time if necessary. Denise thought her employers got more out of people by trusting them in this way.

Is it true what they say about people in advertising getting paid a lot in expenses? Denise said the expenses reimbursed were client lunches, dinner if the staff were working late, trips abroad, and sometimes products for a shoot.

Clients Account Planner

Vanella Hopkins did an HND business studies course at Bristol Polytechnic, specializing in advertising and marketing. This taught her the right vocabulary to use at interviews and she got a job as a graduate trainee in account management in a small agency, called Cherry Hedger Seymour, where she'd previously worked in her school holidays. The agency told her they thought she'd be more suited to account planning and, although she wasn't sure what this was at the time, she took it up and liked it and then moved to Young & Rubicam. This was a very different place – a large, structured agency, with carefully-thought-out systems and a big American influence.

While at Y&R, Vanella was 'head hunted' and taken on by BBH. She had ten interviews to get the job because, BBH told her, 'it's all about people and we want to get to know you before we take you on'. Eventually she passed the 'Sunday lunch' test. This means that the employer, having established a person is good at their job, remembers they are all going to spend a lot of time together and so asks himself: would you invite this person to Sunday lunch?

Vanella thought the claim that the account planner was 'the consumer's voice at the table' was account planners trying to define their role, which is different in every agency. Planners have more time to look at the available data than account handlers, but they don't have a monopoly on the consumer. She thought that she preferred account planning to account handling because she wasn't a person who liked the organizing, or making sure people had done their part of the job, or stage-managing a show. What she did like was presenting to the client and she did this as much as the account handler; she likes looking at piles of data and extracting answers to questions; for example, the Shape yoghurt advertising had been based on good nutrition and low fat for all the family. The sales figures showed that Shape yoghurt was bought by older, dieting women who ate alone. The advertising, therefore, needed to be realigned to the diet-food market; this is very difficult as diet foods, on the whole, have a dreadful image. The only one that has been successful in presenting a positive image is Lean Cuisine. A great deal of interesting material came up in considering all this, such as women's guilt over dieting and bingeing, etc.

Vanella thought that to be in account planning you needed to be excited by advertising. The most fascinating part was the creative process. She liked getting the strategy right and then seeing the advertising she believed in emerge.

Production and Traffic

James Smith first worked in the BBH agency on a holiday job. James enjoyed the job but at the end of the summer decided to go to college to get some more O-levels. He ended up with nine O-levels, plus three CSEs, and then got a phone call from BBH, asking him if he'd like to come back as junior in production.

They talked over his career and whether he should stay in full-time education and do A-levels or start work straight away. In the end, he decided to take the job and has been at BBH for a couple of years.

His department consists of traffic (which estimates, costs, chases up and arranges for the hire of photographers, illustrators, etc.) and production (which deals with the final stages – sending out ads to printers, poster sites, magazines and national newspapers).

James said that 'a good traffic person is never at his desk' (he's around the agency chasing people up) and 'a good production person is always at his desk' (taking the calls from publications, printers, etc.). James has had the chance to work on both as the junior of the department. He has also spent some time in the creative department, as the production department has had a series of students doing work experience. This gave James time to find out about art direction, which interests him.

James thought that this was a department where you couldn't plan anything, because the work was very immediate, and you had to be ready to get up and go and deal with whatever it was necessary to deal with. There might be the internal approval of ads and scripts to organize, involving showing artwork to the creatives, the account handlers and the three partners. He gets to meet and know everyone. He has had to deliver material to places as far away as Belgium, and is constantly chasing people.

James had learned a lot about printing processes and about all the suppliers since he has been in the agency. He has been sent on courses. He'd been to a very good weekend IPA course on traffic and production. He particularly liked this as it involved meeting people from other agencies.

One of the skills in production is knowing the best route to take to get things done. For example, photography is very expensive and so is retouching. The production department will negotiate with the photographer's agent and get to know the different suppliers and get a good relationship with them, for example, by going to see them and explaining the job to them. James thought the day of the production man who was always being taken out to lunch by the suppliers and who would get the printer to do things in a hurry 'as a favour' was over. Production was now more business-like, although they did get entertained by the suppliers at Christmas!

James had originally been interested in advertising because he saw his cousin with a nice car, good clothes and, always jetting off somewhere. It was true people were well paid, but when he got to the agency, he discovered how hard you had to work.

In Conclusion

Several themes kept emerging in my conversations with staff. One was the importance of the three partners named in the title: Bartle, Bogle and Hegarty. These were personally known to all the staff and closely involved in the work.

The second theme was the type of advertising produced and the protection of the creatives and, therefore, the advertising. Their clients had to be people in agreement with their approach and appreciating that it produced good and original advertising.

The third theme was the way the staff was treated, which was to be given freedom to get as much as possible from the job, while at the same time it was accepted that the agency expected a great deal from the staff.

5
Advertising sales

Remember advertising sales

Advertising sales is not usually what people are thinking about when they talk about getting into advertising. Sometimes their faces lengthen when I start talking about advertising sales and they say glumly, 'so you mean tele-sales?'

Do not overlook advertising sales. Why not? Here are four good reasons:

1. You have to be sales-minded for any job in advertising, not just this one with sales in its title.

2. They are usually looking for 20+ recruits. Therefore, it's a possible career for a young adult wanting to change.

3. It's good money, particularly on the national newspapers and ITV stations which are bound by union agreements, or which reflect the value of the salesperson to the company in his or her salary.

4. If you're good at this, you've got the qualities for many other advertising jobs.

Sometimes the word 'sales' is compensated for by the words 'television' and 'newspaper'. These are attractive places to work, but make no mistake, advertising sales is a career in its own right: it's not a way into journalism or television production.

Why advertising sales?

To media owners, advertising is either the only source of revenue or a very important one. For example, some newspapers and magazines are free. The money to produce them comes only from the advertisers. For publications we buy, the advertising revenue is also very important. The income the *Guardian* gets from advertising, for example, exceeds the income from the sales of the paper (i.e. its price).

Newspapers

There are nearly 1,800 newspapers in Britain, both local and national, and they all employ advertising sales staff. Their job is to sell space to clients so that they can advertise in the paper their goods, services and vacancies.

Classified and display

Newspaper advertisements divide into 'classified' and 'display'. Classified advertisements appear under specialized headings (e.g. 'property' or 'vacancies') and although many are small, some are larger and more elaborate and more like 'display' advertisements. For example, a local education authority advertising for a variety of staff may have a large advertisement taking a quarter of a page, with headings and sub-headings and its crest, but this will still count as classified because it appears under a heading.

Display advertisements (sometimes called 'run of paper') are larger and more elaborate, and may fill the whole page of a national newspaper. These advertisements are usually taken by clients with a large advertising budget and their own agency; these clients are often Government departments and national companies.

Telephone and field sales

Much classified sales work is done by telephone. Some of this involves receiving details of vacancies from advertisers who are regular customers of the paper. Some of it is 'canvassing' or 'cold calling', that is contacting potential clients and persuading them of the merits of using one particular newspaper.

There are usually also a few field sales staff in the classified advertising department of a newspaper. This is because major clients often like to meet a salesperson face to face. In display advertising, the work will be mainly field sales, and there will be more contact with agencies, as well as with advertisers.

Magazines

There are even more magazines than newspapers published in this country (7,000 plus). This is because magazines cover a multitude of specialisms, for example trade and technical journals which provide information on a particular industry; or consumer journals which either cover specialist subjects, like photography and records, or are directed at a particular group of people, such as women's magazines, magazines for the retired or the overweight.

Apart from the fact that magazines don't usually have such a clear distinction between classified and display, the work is much the same as on a newspaper. There are telephone and field sales staff and, with a large magazine publisher, sales staff will be allocated to a particular magazine or group of magazines so that they can become familiar with the specialist advertisers.

Above: *Independent's* Classifieds by Tango.
Below: Magazine ad for British Telecom by Bartle, Bogle and Hegarty

Television and radio

The 16 regional ITV companies all carry advertising, as does Channel Four. The companies all have advertising sales offices in London, as well as offices in their own region. They sell 'time' to advertisers, both on their own behalf and on behalf of Channel Four.

Television time sales is the most pressurized and complex of all advertising sales. This is because the cost of time on television is so variable – depending on the time of day, the day of the week, who is likely to be watching and the demand for that particular time from advertisers. Like any commodity, the greater the demand the higher the price and vice versa.

Radio advertising time is sold in a similar way, the main difference being that it is not so expensive or so sought after, and is therefore less pressurized.

Two companies act on behalf of most of the radio stations (Capital Radio in London is the exception and does its own selling). These are Independent Radio Sales and Broadcast Marketing Services. Additionally, the radio stations will sell to local advertisers themselves.

The jobs

There is some variation in these depending on who you're working for. The usual path for people working on newspapers is to start with telephone sales, go on to field sales (either in classified or display) and after this go on to training or management. Magazines are similar. Sometimes people with previous related experience will go directly into field sales.

Television stations have several different levels of jobs in advertising sales, the lowest and often the starting-point, being that of 'traffic clerk'. Once the time has been sold to an advertiser, these people process and log it. This is largely done on a computer. Then come the sales assistants and the sales executives. The sales assistants support the sales executives, doing either the paperwork and/or the telephone sales work, leaving the sales executives free to go out to make presentations and keep contact with the clients. Sales executive jobs can lead to management positions. As well as this, some television companies have market research or marketing departments. It is very important, when selling to the advertiser, to know who is watching your programmes.

What sort of people get in?

Like a lot of advertising, sales is very much a personality business (see Chapter 6). The employers are all looking for the same sort of person. How many of the following adjectives apply to you? Self-confident, energetic, bright, enthusiastic, ebullient, even slightly cheeky. Do you have the will to succeed, guts and drive, get up and go, initiative and the qualities of leadership? There are one or two other points to consider: numeracy is very important, especially in television, where a grasp of figures is crucial. Of course, it is also important to be articulate and in the field sales jobs, well-dressed.

Although these are 'personality' jobs, and the employers often ask for no particular educational qualifications, many of those taken on have A-levels or a degree. This is because employers have a choice of good applicants. The minimum age for most of these posts is 18. The newspapers seldom take anyone under 20, and they prefer a year's experience of work.

How to get a job

When they have advertising sales vacancies, the newspapers advertise in their own pages. The magazine publishers also use newspapers to advertise their vacancies. The television stations do not usually need to advertise, but take up speculative applications, or use word of mouth or staff from advertising agencies. Sometimes they notify vacancies to the careers service.

6

Anatomy of an advertising sales department: The Guardian — Classified Advertising Sales

'You shouldn't bullshit, that's not selling. It's good old assertive behaviour.'

'It's not talking with people, it's not dealing with people, it's selling to people. You're here to make money.'

'Always ask about training. Product, industry and marketing knowledge are very important. Otherwise you're just cannon fodder.'

The Advertising Department

Fiona Morris, deputy advertisement director of the *Guardian*, started as a canvasser ten years ago. A canvasser is a person who sells advertising space over the phone. The tele-sales department is the largest one with 43 staff, field sales having 11 and display 16. Telephone sales is the most cost-effective, as far more employers (it is mainly recruitment advertising) can be contacted by phone in a day than can be visited.

Recruitment

Fiona will advertise in the *Guardian* itself when she wants more staff and the first interviews, are conducted on the telephone. Have applicants read the ad? Are they able to talk about themselves over the phone? If they can't sell themselves, how do they think they can sell the product?

At the face-to-face interview, Fiona may ask applicants to sell her something, like a pen or an ashtray. This is to see if they can come up with some selling-points and whether they're thrown by the question anyway.

Qualities

What sort of person is she looking for? The ideal person will have a sense of humour, resilience, enthusiasm, a good manner, charm, be articulate, intelligent, a good communicator, hard-working and trustworthy.

technology, they will be able to input their ads directly on to a screen and to the printer. At present, the typed ads are sent on the train to Manchester, where the paper is printed.

Helen Bird, Tele-sales person

Helen left school and college well qualified, with 9 O-levels, 2 A-levels and a bilingual secretarial course. As she lived near the *Guardian*, she enquired about secretarial jobs there, and worked as PA/Secretary for Caroline Marland, the advertising director for five years.

She loved the job but there was no career progression. The only progression, secretarially, would be to become the chairman's PA or secretary. The idea of running her own territory in advertising sales

appealed to Helen, so she applied. At the interview she got the classic question of 'how would you sell me this new felt-tip pen?' The interviewer pretended to be a manager from W. H. Smith. Helen said it was surprising how you can come up with reasons for the sale – it would appeal to young people, it came in a good range of bright colours, etc.

Helen was accepted and went on the same two-week training course as Carol. On the Friday afternoon of the second week, she was taken down to the telephone sales room, where she made her first call. She was given Bp–Bz, which is quite an active area as it includes British, Brent and Bristol.

Helen liked the work, although she found the tele-sales room was run in quite a strict way. There were set breaks and chatting was frowned upon. However, conditions were good, the sales people were members of the trade union SOGAT 82, which had negotiated a nine-day fortnight. They work from 9.17 to 5.30 with a 30-minute break in the morning and afternoon and 1¼ hours for lunch (the extra quarter of an hour was so they could get to the canteen in the other building up the road). There's also a small canteen for coffee and sandwiches in their own building.

Helen likes having her own territory, her own baby. She also likes the fact that the more you do, the more you earn. There is a bonus system, and how much bonus you get depends on whether you reach your target or go beyond it. She also likes the deadlines. Thursdays and Fridays are hectic days because they are the deadlines for Mondays and Tuesdays. She likes the busy-ness and the activity, and the fact that you are able to think for yourself rather than carry out someone else's orders. There is nothing in particular she dislikes. There are bad days, but she finds difficult people a challenge – she was used to dealing with difficult people who rang up to complain when she was a secretary.

Helen would like to do face-to-face selling eventually. She wouldn't mind doing a stint as a trainer first, and said that the *Guardian* was a very good company for promoting from within.

Field and Display Sales

The field staff should be out of the office most of the time. They are responsible for a geographical area, for example, north-east towards Cambridge, or south-east towards Kent.

Display staff specialise in certain products, for example, building societies. The person dealing with building societies may go north for a week to visit the societies based there (the Bradford & Bingley, the Halifax, etc.).

Both display and field staff must be prepared to spend time away from home, and must be self-motivated as the job can be lonely. You have to set out early, find the place you're visiting, find somewhere to park, and negotiate the one-way system in a strange town. You may go down to the dining-room in the hotel and find that you're the only person there. On the plus side, the field and display staff get invited by their customers to plenty of Friday-night drink-ups and leaving do's but they have to be careful with drinking and driving. This type of selling is a job with its own life-style.

Carol Stewart, Field Sales staff

Carol had worked as a telephone sales supervisor at Virgin Records, as an interviewer at Atlas Recruitment, and as a receptionist at a classical music publisher, before she applied for her job at the *Guardian*.

She was attracted by a line in the advertisement which asked 'Can you sell me this space?' It was a challenge which she took up. She was also, and still is, a *Guardian* reader.

First of all, she had a group interview, which she found quite daunting. The interviewers would pounce on people and ask them questions like 'If you could choose to go out to lunch with anyone you wanted, who would it be?' In the end, she decided that they were looking for someone with individuality who could cope with that sort of a situation. After she'd had her one-to-one interview, the *Guardian* told her she'd got the job.

She started two weeks later with a group of ten people, who still keep in contact although some have left. The two-week training course was 'the best sales training I've ever had'. It covered sales technique, the history of the paper, and included some role play which was recorded and played back to them. At the end, they were introduced to the department.

Carol had the letter F, and all advertisers with this as their first letter were put through to her. This is when the nerves really start. However, there is continuing training during the first week, with the trainer able to plug into the calls to give feedback and help.

After two weeks, Carol sold her first space as a result of cold calling. 'There's screaming and shouting and jubilation when someone sells their first lead,' she said. What she liked about telephone sales was the great atmosphere, 'like a family', in a big open plan office with something always going on. 'You're terrified at first, but once you've made a few calls you realize you've got the upper hand. You get to speak to some lovely people and get to know your regular clients, and have to push yourself to talk about work sometimes, as you just want to have a chat to them', said Carol.

Sometimes the cold calls could turn out unpleasant, and she'd think, 'don't talk to me like that, I'm a human being'. People can be extremely offensive sometimes. But a good aspect of the job was that you're left to run your own territory, and when you're going on holiday, you let all your regular customers know – although there is a system for covering if you're away.

Carol was in telephone sales for a year and one month, when her trainer suggested she applied for a vacancy that had come up in field sales. Carol was quite happy in what she was doing and hadn't thought of moving, but she considered the suggestion, talked it over with her family and boy-friend and decided to give it a go. She got the

job and it was back to training again, starting with a refresher of the previous course, and then on to the techniques of face-to-face selling – studying body language, for example, and the role playing again.

Then it was time for Carol's first face-to-face client ('which was awful,' she said) and she got up in good time, put on her favourite outfit and had her hair looking immaculate. Then she went out into what seemed liked a Force 9 gale with wind, rain, the lot, and arrived at the client's (which was the Royal Borough of Kensington and Chelsea) wet through. However, her trainer went with her, as she did for the first four or five appointments, and after that Carol felt confident on her own.

Now she's usually in the office on Mondays and part of Friday, and out all the rest of the time. She deals with local authorities in south-east England, covering London and the south coast as far as Winchester and Hampshire and as far north as Northampton.

It's necessary to have some field reps as the bigger clients prefer personal contact. Carol mainly uses the visits to keep the clients up to date, telling them the readership figures and making them aware of what the *Guardian* has to offer.

Carol would get a car but she can't drive, although she is learning. There is a pool of four or five cars which the staff can use when necessary.

Carol thought the minus side of her new job was the weather – in the winter, when it was snowing and raining, she didn't like going out of the office a lot. However, there were a lot of pluses. These were: getting out to meet people, fewer people being horrible to her, easier selling as she became more and more knowledgeable about the product and the market-place. It is also easier to sell when you can put something in front of the client: even a piece of paper saying how many readers the paper has is more effective than saying the same thing on the phone. It's also easier to put your personality across face to face.

Carol isn't contemplating leaving her job at the moment, although in the long term she is interested in marketing. Her manager told her that it takes a year to get used to the job, a year to get the upper hand and a year to enjoy it, and that is what she will probably do.

7
Getting jobs in advertising

Finding the vacancies and getting in

Suppose you have read this book so far and have decided advertising is for you, what do you do next?

Think back to Chapter 3, and remember the numbers of people employed in advertising agencies. It's a tiny number compared with banking or the retail business. Even if you add the numbers employed on advertising in the marketing departments of companies or on advertising sales (and these numbers are more difficult to pin down) it's not a big industry.

It's also an industry with a very attractive image. So, put together the small numbers of people employed and the glamour associated with advertising and you can see why entry to this business is so competitive. For this reason, job vacancies are not necessarily **advertised**, so one of the methods of entry is proposing yourself to the prospective employer or making **speculative applications**.

Advertised Vacancies for Graduates

This is the most clear-cut method of entry into the business. Every year the leading agencies recruit between them around 120 graduate trainees. Some of them issue information about their graduate recruitment. This can also be useful to non-graduates wanting to find out about the agencies. Some agencies do the 'milk round' to the universities; others just rely on the letters they inevitably receive from graduates.

It's worth pointing out that, although graduates have the advantage of a clear path into advertising, there are thought to be 600 to 1,500 applicants in any one year looking for a trainee place. This figure is uncertain, although 1,500 is the number usually quoted.

Likewise, the sales departments of the national newspaper advertise from time to time in their own pages for sales trainees. These advertisements are not usually specifically for graduates, but are either for graduates or for people of 20 plus with work experience.

The advertisers, like the agencies, appoint graduate trainees to their marketing departments, to the marketing trainee posts, of which advertising can be one part. Again like the agencies, marketing departments offer a definite graduate-trainee method of entry, and can pick and choose because marketing too is seen as a glamour area.

Advertised Vacancies for School-leavers

Suppose, however, you are leaving school at 16, 17 or 18 and want to apply. Are there equivalent training schemes for you?

The answer is 'No'. Agencies do not have a 'school-leaver' training scheme in the same way that they have a graduate-training scheme. The school-leavers are too young for most of the posts the graduates will fill (usually account executives jobs), and the agencies wouldn't know what to do with them for three years while they matured. Therefore, the advertised vacancies for school-leavers are for specific jobs which the young person can do immediately and make a contribution, as, for example, post-room/print-room messenger, receptionist/telephonist, secretary, media assistant, media research assistant, information assistant and so on. These jobs vary depending on the agency, but they fall into three main categories:

1. Typing jobs: secretary, receptionist, typist, etc.

2. 'Go-fer' jobs: messenger/assistant in the print room or production.

3. Junior/assistant jobs: junior in the media department, the information or production departments.

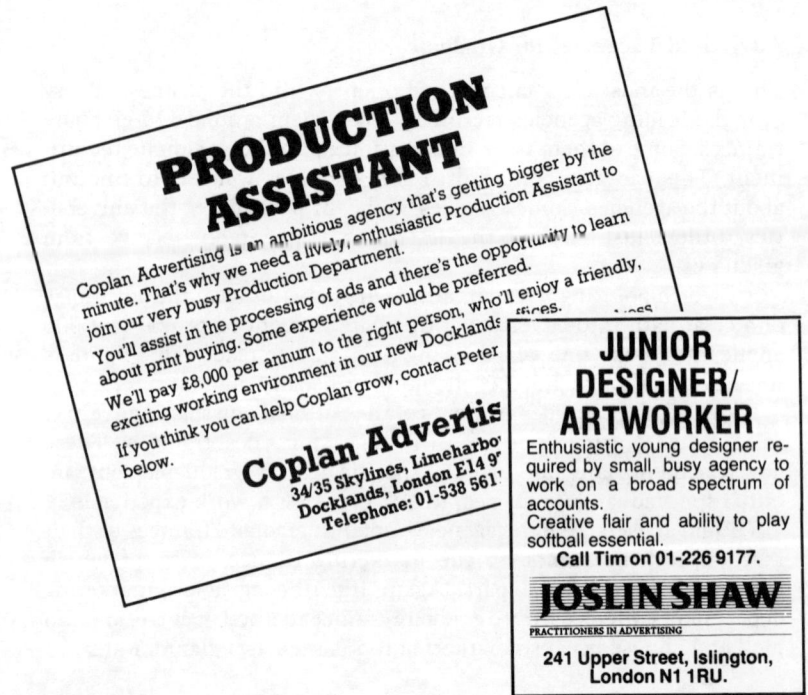

Most school-leavers would like to get into the junior/assistant-type jobs. Don't only go for these because there're not very many of them; anyway they often incorporate either typing or running errands. For example, the junior in the media department is more useful if he or she can type, and may be expected to run errands anyway.

It's worth mentioning typing again, because keyboard skills are very useful in advertising, as they now are in so many jobs. Learning to type or wordprocess or to know how to operate a computer terminal or microcomputer is a useful asset. If you can, you will find there are far more jobs you can apply for in advertising. This doesn't mean you have to be a typist or a secretary; it simply means you've mastered one of the tools which is used in the office.

Occasionally, vacancies may be advertised for younger people in advertising sales: not usually to be the sales person but to give the clerical/administrative support to the sales person. Vacancies for school-leavers in the advertising section of an advertiser are even more rarely seen. Sometimes, there will be one for a junior in the marketing department, often incorporating figure work and often not much to do with advertising.

Speculative Applications

As in any popular area of employment, people don't apply only to advertised vacancies, or apply only to established graduate-training schemes. They write to companies in the hope that a suitable vacancy will occur, or even that their letter will be so impressive that one will be made for them!

Most companies use their speculative applications. After all, it's the cheapest recruiting method of all. The employer doesn't have to do anything except look at the letters and CVs as they arrive and if a vacancy arises, match the applicant to it. Graduates should not fight shy of this method either. If they write to agencies (not only the top 20 with training schemes), they may not get a grand graduate-training post but they might get an older version of one of the school-leaver, trainee-type posts – especially if they can type and are prepared to do anything. School-leavers should also use this method. I remember a girl who applied to a vacancy I told her about (an information assistant at J. Walter Thompson). She was late applying because I'd only just met her and I'd had the vacancy some time already, but she said she'd have a go. Indeed, JWT had already appointed someone else who failed to turn up on the day, so my candidate got the job. The chances of striking lucky like this may be remote, but if she had not contacted the company, there would have been no chance at all. The same applies to speculative letters.

If you are an adult wanting a change of career, you have an even harder problem. The most likely area for you to enter, if you have a few years' work experience and the right personality, is advertising sales. Apart from this it's going to be difficult without some relevant experience or training. Therefore, it's particularly important to present a good CV and covering letter, drawing out in your application your greatest selling points.

Do Research

Particularly if you are a graduate, you will be asked questions about the agency. Not only will you be asked who the agency's clients are, but you may well be asked what you think of the advertising campaigns for these clients. So, really two levels of research are necessary:

1. Finding out the facts – as many as you can about your prospective employer. Who are the founder members, partners or leading executives of the agency? Who are the clients? What sort of advertising have they done? What is the agency's 'character'? Is it known as 'creative led', or is it particularly strong on account planning and marketing?

2. Forming your own opinions. This is more difficult and does not happen at will. What you can do is start asking yourself 'Is that a good advertisement?' when you see advertisements on the TV or in the paper. If not, why not? And if it is, why? Do *you* like it? If so, is this because it's aimed at your sex/age group/class, and it works? Or do you like it because it's funny and/or aesthetically pleasing, and do you remember the *name* of the product? However enjoyable or beautiful the advertisement is, it dooon't work if you don't receive the message and associate it with the product. Why did they make it that way? Who will it appeal to? After a bit of this, and reading the trade magazine and this book, you should be well away. In fact, research shows (as they say) that contemporary young people are very aware of how advertising works and even know the vocabulary used.

Prepare a Good *Curriculum Vitae* (CV)

This is a sheet of paper giving the prospective employer details about you. It's a very useful thing to have anyway. More and more employers ask for a CV now instead of using an application form, and, of course, it's essential for your speculative applications.

The younger you are, the shorter it will be. A school-leaver may be able to get everything on one side of an A4 sheet; a graduate or an

THE CURRICULUM VITAE OF MARY JO BLACKSMITH

Personal
Address	94, Poets Road, London N5 2HF
Telephone	01-359-6789
Date of Birth	1st April 1970
Marital Status	Single
Nationality	British

Education and Qualifications
Establishments Attended	Highbury High School 1981-1986
	Kingsway Princeton College 1986-1988
Examinations Passed	GCE 'O' levels in English Language,
	Mathematics, French, Art & Needlework.
	GCE 'A' levels in English and Art.
	RSA II in Typing.

Other Activities and Interests
At School	I was editor of the 5th year magazine and wrote most of it. I enjoyed acting and singing in 'Joseph and the Amazing Technicolour Dreamcoat'. (I was a brother).
At College	I took evening classes in typing and wordprocessing.
Otherwise	I collect 50s and 60s clothes, go swimming and enjoy socialising.

Work Experience
Marks & Spencer	1986-1988 I worked in the busy Marble Arch branch on Saturdays as a sales assistant.
Burger Delight	Summer 1987 I worked as a waitress/cashier.

Referees
Mrs Boston Smith,	Mr Ahandi,
Headmistress,	Manager,
Highbury High School,	Burger Delight,
Lower Greek Street,	46, Upper Street,
London N5 6VP	London N1 3BU

A school leaver's CV

adult will probably need two sides. Unless you have a lot of experience, or are applying to be the managing director, try to keep it to two sides.

There are two aspects to a CV, as to any form of communication, the presentation and the content.

The content should be clear, concise and include all possible selling-points. Then, presentation should be smart and clear. If you're really very artistic or imaginative, you can do something original with the presentation. However, many people who attempt to do this fail, and the result is simply embarrassing (see 'Tales of graduate recruitment' at the end of this chapter). Len Barkey at Saatchi's once received an application in the form of a wellington boot, and a colleague of mine who deals with art and design careers received a CV in the form of a painting. Whether these people got jobs depended on the content of the CV, however, and how they performed at interviews.

Some of the content of a CV is quite straightforward: your name and address, date of birth, educational qualifications, etc. Include also anything else relevant, such as Saturday jobs, holiday jobs, outside activities, extra-school activities. Don't write long paragraphs about these. Keep then brief and highlight your initiative activity. Use active verbs: I *organized* the school fête; I *edited* the college magazine.

Should you type your CV or handwrite it? Unless your handwriting is very beautiful and very clear, you should type it or get it typed. It will then photocopy better, and you are going to need lots of copies when you send off your speculative applications.

A final thought about CVs. Some dedicated people do different ones for different types of companies, and this can pay off. The idea is that it pays to emphasize different points to different companies. Probably, this is more valuable to a person with some employment experience, who has more points to select from, or possibly a graduate who has been very active at polytechnic or university.

The Covering Letter

This is the more usual place to point out any particularly relevant experience. 'I am applying to your company because ...'. The covering letter is important; it's not a sort of a compliment slip. Carefully think out why you are applying, why it's worth their while considering you for employment, and write it down. Ask the firm to consider you for any suitable current vacancies, or to keep you in mind for any which may occur in the future.

The Interview

Try a simple exercise. Take a piece of paper and write down, without stopping to think, five important things about going for an interview. Now read on.

I did this, and my five important things were:

1. Get there on time

2. Look smart, neat and tidy

3. Do your homework about the company

4. Ask questions and reply fluently

5. Smile!

There are a couple of additional points about interviews in advertising, particularly: agencies are looking for determination, commitment and good communication. So the person who rings back or even calls in when they haven't heard the outcome of the interview is perceived to be the persistent one. (Be persistent politely, of course.) If an agency asks you to write in, or bring a CV, you must do so; communication is what the business is all about. You may find that the employers do not always behave as well as you do in the keeping-people-informed stakes. No one is perfect, and sometimes they are slow or forgetful in letting people know the results of an interview. The fact that not many agencies have personnel departments, and the recruitment is often done by departmental heads who are busy with other things, doesn't help.

You may find this all a bit off-putting. So many things to think about to get an interview, let alone a job! However, if you're the right type for advertising, it's worth going ahead and making the effort. Agencies are open to talent and to young people. If you have the right abilities and you persist, you will probably get in eventually, if not immediately. Agencies are often very good at passing on candidates they can't take themselves, but who they think are good, to other agencies, so it's worth getting to the interviews.

Check-list of Things to Do

1. Contact the notifiers of vacancies in your area: the Career Service, Job Centres, employment agencies.

2. Look in papers and trade magazines for vacancies.

3. Write to employers: a good covering letter with a CV enclosed. A list of agencies, and advertisers is to be found in the *Advertisers' Annual*.

4. Get your CV ready and make sure it's good; Ditto the covering letter.

5. Research the companies you are applying to.

6. Prepare for the interview, if necessary by getting someone to give you a mock interview.

Tales of graduate recruitment

During my years of dealing with advertising careers, I've talked to many agencies about their graduate recruitment. It seems a good idea to spend the last half of this chapter describing the procedures used in some detail, and why people fail at each stage.

Making the Application

Each year, there are around 120 trainee vacancies for graduates in the major advertising agencies. The number any agency takes on fluctuates, and some years they may not recruit anyone, but they usually look for a small number, say four to six trainees.

The applications start coming in to the agencies as early as October, and they may have a cut-off date as early as January, doing their final selection in March or April. Therefore it's important for the undergraduates to start their preparation for application more than a year ahead.

Most of the agencies will accept a CV and covering letter, or the standard university/polytechnic application form with a covering letter. J. Walter Thompson have their own application form which is likely to put off those not seriously interested, as applicants are asked to give a brief history of themselves, describe the milestones in their lives and comment on two advertisements, as well as answer all the usual questions about academic achievement and work experience.

Undergraduates can get the literature and information about the major advertising agencies from their Careers Advisory Services, or write to the agencies direct. Some agencies also do the milk round, although usually to selected universities only.

It's worth mentioning at this stage that some agencies consider non-graduates of around the same age-group (early twenties) along with their graduate applicants. These can be staff in the agency (e.g. production assistants or secretaries) who want to become account executives, or people with a few years' work experience in a different business.

Stage One: The Paper Sift

Why don't some candidates get to the interview stage? It has nothing whatever to do with which degree subject they studied. Agencies always quote examples of theologians and archaeologists who have made excellent account executives. A degree in media studies is not necessarily an advantage; indeed, I've heard it said that it produces people who purport to know about 'the media' but have little useful knowledge of advertising.

No, the application forms or CVs are often turned down for very simple reasons: a low standard of literacy shown by illegibility, messiness, poor expression and lousy spelling. Applicants must be able to speak and write logically and coherently. Flashy or funny-but-not-funny applications do not help a lot. Bad covering letters are a frequent reason for rejection: one agency said the covering letter was more important than the CV.

Apart from this, it helps if the candidate shows a commitment to advertising as a career, some interest and enthusiasm for it, and can give a plausible reason for applying to a particular agency.

There is usually no set proportion of applicants interviewed. One agency divided the applicants into 'good, possible, maybe and no', and started by interviewing the goods and the possibles. If too many of these turned out to be non-starters (could it be some people get friends to write their applications for them?), they would move on to the maybes.

The First Interview

Most agencies have a two-interview system, inviting a minority of the first interviewees back for a second interview or more elaborate selection days.

The first interview is a chance for the agency to assess the personality of the candidate and to gauge his or her commitment and enthusiasm for the career. The person unable to discuss ads, who had done no homework about the agency and who does not display the required personal qualities (see Chapter 3) is unlikely to get any further.

The Second Interview

This can be quite elaborate, and often involves some sort of group activity in which the candidates can be observed relating to others. Usually only a small number (20 to 25) will get to this stage, which may include social events, and one or two days of group exercises.

Usually the groups are observed by a 'minder', who makes copious notes of who did and said what. Often the group is asked to produce a brief for an advertising campaign, usually for a client the agency already has.

These are testing procedures, but most of the candidates who have got this far are likely to be employable in agencies anyway. Indeed, the agencies are often helpful in giving feedback to those they don't take on, telling them where they went wrong. Many of the finalists may also be finalists or interviewees with other agencies.

Who succeeded

After the final selections have been made, is it possible to draw any conclusions about who succeeded and why? There are two main points which have been made elsewhere in the book, but are certainly worth making again.

1. *Preparation*. The people who had visited agencies for a chat, attended milk round presentations, followed up any personal contacts in advertising, read the trade Press, and obtained information both from the agencies and their Careers Advisory Service, stood the best chance of getting through the selection procedure.

2. *Personality*. See Chapter 3 again. Remember especially that an acute sense of commercialism is very important. Someone who is interested in the way a business works and is 'excited by selling one more case of baked beans tomorrow' is likely to succeed. The account executives act as advisers to clients and must question their decisions and attitudes, and how they run some aspects of their business. They need to be mature as their clients are frequently older than they are. They also need to be quite obsessively interested in advertising.

8
Courses and qualifications

People often ask me 'What course should I do to get into advertising?' Perhaps they think that advertising is something like engineering or medicine, where you need particular qualifications to learn the trade and then go on to practise it.

The answer is you don't. There are various courses and qualifications which can be very useful, but none of them are essential. I remember reading an article in *Campaign* about a successful copywriter who had had an excellent background for his job, it said: he'd been a used-car salesman.

Apart from 'the academy of the world' and used-car selling, what else can you do? This chapter covers the relevant courses and qualifications, giving more detail about the two copy-writing courses, which are the only two at present, and explaining about some other qualifications and official bodies. It also mentions a few other colleges which are involved in advertising.

Watford College: the copy-writing course

Watford has advertising courses both on the copywriting side and on the business side. They are not courses which offer nationally recognized qualifications and this can make it difficult to get a grant. However, they are still very useful.

The copy-writing course has been going for 27 years and is the longest-running advertising course in Britain. The candidates are usually in the 18 to 26 age-range, although they have had a few older ones. Between 60 and 80 people apply every year from all over the country, Scotland, Bristol, Wales and Ireland for example. They have very few local people. All applicants get a form and a leaflet and if they return the completed form they do a copy test. From this they decide who to interview and generally end up with 16 people accepted on the course and a waiting-list of 10 to 15 people in case anyone drops out. A typical year's intake might include a good mix of graduates, schoolleavers and people who have some experience of work but are now determined to get into advertising. All must have 2 A-levels (including English) and there are only occasional exceptions to this. Graduates can be in any subject – archaeology, geology, history; they don't particularly look for English graduates.

Student work from Hounslow College by Mercedes Morgan and James Sexton
See page 7 for credits.

Course Content

In the first few weeks, there are lectures on various aspects of advertising. These include media and marketing lectures, plus an introduction to layout and graphic design. The students also write ads from the very first day. The staff give them a lot of work and try to make the briefs as realistic as possible.

In the second term, there are more outside visitors, frequently creative directors or writers now in middle or senior positions, who've been on the course previously.

The aim is to get each student equipped with a portfolio which is worth showing round the London agencies. To do this, they will complete a large number of briefs and end up with several strong campaigns in their portfolios.

Placements

Watford has good support from certain agencies – mainly the top 20 or 30 London ones.

Some agencies say 'Yes we will have a student,' but set a competition so they can get the pick of the bunch. J. Walter Thompson have done this for the past three years. Other agencies may specifically ask for someone not inept, or others for a team (an art director or copy-writer). This isn't always easy, as not all the graphic design students want to get into advertising, and also the copy-writer and art director have to get on with each other. However, Watford does co-operate with a number of art colleges to form teams towards the end of each academic year.

Course Assessment

They have two external assessors appointed by the IPA, one from a consumer agency and one from an industrial/technical agency. These see the diploma work and all the course work as well. The assessors and the course supervisor generally agree on what the diploma grade should be.

Grants

Fifty per cent of the students manage to get a grant. This depends on the education authority, as it is discretionary.

Jobs

The course is geared to getting people into jobs and the tutors try to give people as many introductions to agencies as possible. At one time, the agencies would offer the students permanent jobs where

Dr. martens steel toe caps.

The Indestructable Dr. Marten.

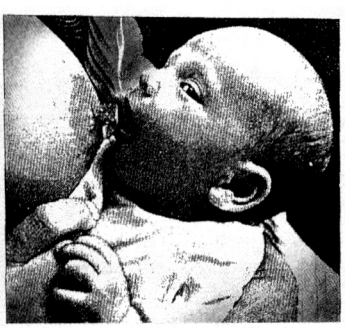

THERE'S SOMETHING ADDICTIVE
ABOUT THIS MOTHER'S MILK.

A Mother breast-feeding baby should be the most ... thing in the world. ... of course, the mother ... Not only does smoking ... to inadequate breast ... reduction, but nicotine has ... found in the breast milk ... where who smoke. Even then, ... first taste of nicotine may ... before this; in the womb.

An unborn child absorbs ... nicotine than the smoking ... -to-be. Also the mother

inhales various poisons from her cigarettes including carbon monoxide, which deprive the baby of oxygen. Furthermore, smoking during pregnancy causes a two-fold increase in the risk of spontaneous abortion, and babies born to women who smoke are on average 200 grammes lighter than babies of non-smoking mothers.

But babies aren't the only ones who suffer from other people's cigarette smoke, for it

kills 1000 adult non-smokers every year. You should be more considerate where and when you smoke. You could start by not damaging or even killing your own baby. After all, if you don't care about the health of your own child, how are you going to be considerate towards anyone else?

KEEP YOUR SMOKE TO YOURSELF.

Jebsens
ST COMPANY REPORT

Student work from
Hounslow College.
See page 7 for credits.

they had their attachments, but recently they have become much more wary about committing themselves. Usually, the majority of the students are placed by the January/February following the summer they leave. Mostly, they want to go to the leading London agencies and this can make finding a job a longer process.

Hounslow College

Hounslow College has run a graphic design course with an advertising option for many years. Several years ago, it introduced a parallel copy-writing course into the art department. This gives the opportunity for potential copy-writers and art directors to pair up while on the course, on their placements in industry, and when job-seeking at the end.

These courses are both two-year Higher Business and Technical Education Council (BTEC) Diplomas and the relevant entry require-ments apply. Those on the graphic design diploma need to have a BTEC graphic design or similar; those on the copy-writing course usually have 1 A-level and 4 GCSEs. English is useful and so is art.

Some graduates take the copy-writing course, as do some older people. The college once had a girl with an English degree who'd been taken on at a prestigious agency as a graduate trainee in account handling. She decided she didn't want that, but did want to be a copy-writer and supported herself on the Hounslow course, getting into copy-writing at the end.

There are around 150 applicants for both courses, of whom about 50 are for copy-writing, which has a maximum of 14 students. There are 24 on the graphics/art direction course.

As well as presenting their academic qualifications, the students take a copy test and are interviewed. It is very important they understand what copy-writing is.

Content

Once on the course, the students study the theory of advertising, and the basic art direction skills of hand-lettering, layout, working out where copy goes, etc. They are set advertising briefs, and enter competitions with other colleges. They hear talks from visitors on topics such as marketing, the work of the account executive and, most importantly, copy-writing. Students also go out on placements to three or four different agencies in the two years (in pairs with an art director). It's difficult to get the placements in the agencies and the college staff have to work at it. Some of the agencies the students go to are Ogilvy & Mather, Saatchi & Saatchi, Boase Massimi Pollitt, and Hedger Mitchells Sark.

Getting a Job

Students get their folders for the Christmas of the second year, and then visit prospective employers, getting their 'book' reviewed. The book will contain five or six campaigns with two or three ads in each. The big agencies will be looking at the quality of the ideas. They aren't worried about how crudely the book is 'roughed out'. The more middle-weight agencies require more finished graphics.

Some students get a job quickly after the end of the course. Others can take more than a year. This is because some are willing to work only at top-flight agencies and refuse jobs which are offered to them in others. Most students stay in London (indeed, they were advised to do so) and later move to an agency elsewhere if they wanted to.

Pairs

Pairing off the students is by no means easy. 'A bit like a marriage agency,' said one tutor. For one thing, not all graphics students will choose to follow the advertising option, so there are likely to be some copy-writing students left over unpaired. Then the pairs can quarrel, separate, or reform as other pairs in different combinations. This, of course, also happens in the agency, with the copy-writer and art director falling out and having tremendous arguments, but always uniting against the account executive and the client: then 'it's back to back'.

Which ever way you look at it it s still wrong !

Imagine being taken out of your natural environment, and kept in a small age.
Imagine being trapped for days, and your only means of escape is to gnaw through your own limbs.
Imagine being cut with a knife and skinned alive.

Imagine going through all this just for somebody elses vanity.
Thousands of animals go through this for yours.
LYNX are an action group striving to stop the merciless killing of fur bearing animals. We need your support.

Once they've got in, there is tremendous scope for copy-writers. Some go freelance, others are offered jobs by the agency's clients and move 'across the tracks'. They can go on to become the creative director in an agency.

And finally ...

What makes a good copy-writer? That's what everyone wants to know. Copy-writers certainly need imagination and a lot of talent. In the big agencies, where there's a lot of television advertising, the copy-writer is really working in a branch of entertainment. The viewers expect the ads to be as good as, or better than, the programmes, and these advertisements are generally humorous. For this, the agencies are looking for someone 'very slightly lunatic', who can tackle things in a fresh way.

CAM Education Foundation

This is the only organization which runs professional training courses for advertising. CAM stands for Communication Advertising and Marketing. The foundation was set up in 1969 to run examinations for the advertising industry. Since then it has not had a smooth ride, for the IPA, which represents the major advertising agencies, withdrew its support from the examination system, and now runs its own training courses for staff from member-agencies. However, CAM has updated its syllabus and survived. Indeed, there is no exact equivalent of CAM and it has around 3,000 students registered at present.

The Certificate and Diploma

In the certificate course there is a wide range of subjects: marketing, advertising, public relations, media, research and behavioural studies, communication practice and business and economic environment. Six of these have to be passed to get the certificate. The diploma is designed for people who want to specialize in a particular area, that is public relations or advertising, and the papers can be chosen accordingly.

The Courses

Most CAM courses are taken as evening classes. The College for the Distributive Trades in London is one of the few colleges which has a half-day release course. Outside London, the courses are frequently taken by correspondence. There are also some small private colleges

Smoke twenty cigarettes and your baby drinks the nicotine from seven.

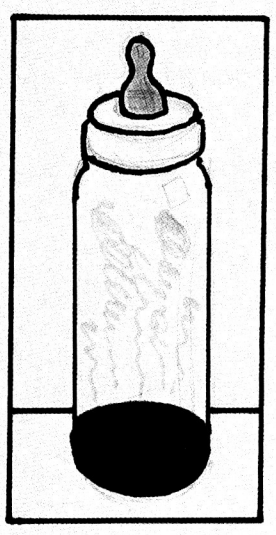

keep smoking to yourself. Ash.

which have been set up by people in the industry (their results and standards vary). Overseas students often attend these colleges.

Exemptions

It's possible to gain exemptions from the CAM exams by taking certain Business and Technician Education Council (BTEC) diplomas and degrees in business studies with an option in advertising/ marketing.

Entry Qualifications

To register for the exams, students must be at least 18, and usually are expected to have five GCEs, including two A-level passes or the equivalent. Those with one year's relevant work experience are accepted with five O-levels or GCSEs, and exceptions can sometimes be made for those with a minimum of three years' experience in the business.

Why Sit These Exams?

When it's not compulsory in the advertising industry, why sit the CAM exams? There are two main reasons:
1. People who are working in an advertising agency in a 'support' capacity, say as a secretary or a junior in the production department, take the exams to prove how keen they are and to show that they have a commitment to the industry and want to be taken seriously when it comes to career progression.
2. People take the exams to widen their theoretical knowledge. You might be working in a public relations consultancy and know all about it but want more detailed knowledge of advertising or marketing so that, when you come across them, you understand how these work.

So Finally ...

Advertising is not a very theoretical subject. Attempts to produce a degree in advertising have failed. All the same, my personal view is that it would be a loss if no set of examinations for the business existed at all, for the reasons outlined above. In any occupation, some theoretical knowledge is valuable.

BTEC courses, degrees and other 'business' advertising courses

The subject which comes nearest to being relevant to advertising careers (disregarding the specialist courses for copywriting and art direction) is business studies.

There are some business studies degree and Higher National Diploma (HND) courses which cover advertising and/or marketing as an option (more usually marketing). For example, the College for the Distributive Trades in London runs an HND course in business studies which covers such subjects as advertising, public relations and marketing. If they wish, the students can pick their options so that they have a very advertising-orientated package. Southampton Institute of Higher Education has a two-year Diploma in Communication Studies, which is creatively orientated and covers advertising, marketing, public relations and media planning. The Institute is applying for approval from the Business and Technician Education Council (BTEC) to run this as an HND course.

Watford College runs two advertising 'business' courses: a six-month course for graduates and a one-year course for students with A-levels. These are their own courses, very much geared to grooming people for employment in the advertising world by helping them to understand and experience it.

A full list of business studies courses and their options is available from the Council for National Academic Awards (CNAA) (degrees) and BTEC (Higher National Diplomas). Addresses are given in the 'Useful Addresses' section at the end of the book.

Specialist Courses and Other Degrees/Diplomas

Although business studies is the nearest academic subject to advertising, in looking for graduate trainees, the advertising agencies don't care greatly about the type of degree. It's the person they look at. Graduates may have degrees in fine art or physics, just as much as the more apparently relevant business studies degree.

HND versus Degree

This is another factor to consider. Again agencies vary, as they do in so many ways. Some will consider HND students alongside graduates (Saatchi & Saatchi for example are liberal-minded about this), others will not. So, is it worth doing a specialist course like the HND at the College for the Distributive Trades in London? It will be of no use if you don't have the right personality in the first place. In may cases, it will not get you interviewed as a prospective graduate trainee. On the plus side, it will give you a lot of knowledge which will help you to make well-informed applications. It could get you into one-off vacancies, rather than into a graduate-trainee scheme.

The Institute of Marketing's exams

As marketing and advertising are closely linked, it's worth mentioning the exams of the institute. Someone working in an advertising agency would be unlikely to take those, but staff working in the marketing department of an advertiser might. The Institute of Marketing is not only an examining body, but also exists to promote the profession.

Like CAM the institute gives exemption from its examinations to those who have completed approved business studies courses. For further details of its courses, write to the institute address on page 95.

Graphic design courses

This is a large subject in its own right. For further information, see *Getting Jobs in Graphics* by Terry Jones. I mention the courses here because this is the route which will be taken by the art director.

Art colleges throughout the country offer a variety of graphic-design courses. There are either degrees or diplomas validated by BTEC. Most courses give opportunities to specialize in various aspects of graphics, including art direction. Hounslow and Watford have the advantage of copy-writing courses in parallel or in association with them. Two of the lecturers from Hounslow College have recently moved to Amersham College and are planning to develop the advertising aspect of the graphics courses there.

The School of Communications Arts

It's also worth mentioning this independent college which runs courses particularly geared to the needs of the advertising business. It was set up by John Gillard, an experienced art school teacher who wanted to provide better training for creatives in advertising. It provides 40 students with an intensive one-year course. The course is supported by many of the leading people in advertising, who set projects for the students. The problem is that it costs £5,700 a year, although loans with low repayment rates have been arranged with the Midland Bank.

Advertising bodies

There are various associations of employers in the advertising business, representing different sectors. The two most useful to mention in this book are the Institute of Practitioners in Advertising (IPA) and the Advertising Association (AA).

The Institute of Practitioners in Advertising (IPA)

This is the body which represents the major advertising agencies. It deals with any big and controversial issues on behalf of the agencies. It runs various services, such as training courses and a library. It produces statistics on numbers employed by their member-firms. It's a larger, wealthier organization than CAM or the AA, and although it has more money and status, it also does a lot of heart-searching about its role. (Heart-searching about your role is characteristic of the business.)

The Advertising Association (AA)

This represents *all* the various interests in the advertising industry. It represents all three sectors – the advertisers, the agencies and the media. If a view is asked for that concerns the whole business, the reply will come from the AA. If, however, it concerns only the agencies, it will come from the IPA. If two or more of the sectors in the business are at variance, the AA won't touch it either. They must both express their own views.

It's the AA which has produced a careers booklet on behalf of the industry.

The Designers and Art Directors Association (DADA)

DADA is an organization which aims to maintain and raise standards of creativity and design. It gives awards for various categories of advertising and runs evening classes for people wanting to get into advertising. These are mainly taken by people from art school, although anyone able to benefit can apply, say someone with a little experience in the business already. The students are set briefs by various agencies and move round to six agencies of a cartel of 24, working a brief and then having it criticized by the agency's creative team. This is a quick and controlled way to produce work, and useful for those wanting to produce a 'book' to show to agencies.

Useful addresses

The Advertising Association (AA)
Abford House
15 Wilton Road
London SW1V 1NJ

Amersham College of Further
Education, Art and Design
Stanley Hill
Amersham
Buckinghamshire HP7 9HN

The Association of
Media Independents
23 Darmouth Park Avenue
London NW5 1JL

Business and Technician
Education Council (BTEC)
Central House
Upper Woburn Place
London WC1A 0HH

City of London Polytechnic
84 Moorgate
London EC2M 6SQ

College for the Distributive
Trades
30 Leicester Square
London WC2

Communication Advertising
and Marketing,
Education Foundation (CAM)
15 Wilton Road
London SWN 1NJ

Council for National
Academic Awards (CNAA)
344–354 Gray's Inn Road
London WC1X 8BP

Designers & Art Directors
Association (DADA)
12 Carlton House Terrace
London SW1Y 5AH

Hounslow Borough Council
London Road
Isleworth
Middlesex TW7 4HA

The Institute of Marketing
Moor Hall
Cookham
Berkshire SL6 9QU

The Institute of Practitioners
in Advertising (IPA)
44 Belgrave Square
London SW1X 8QS

The School of
Communication Arts
Woodbridge House
9 Haywards Place
London EC1

Southampton Institute of
Higher Education
East Park Terrace
Southampton SO9 4WW

Watford College
Hempstead Road
Watford
Hertfordshire WD1 3EZ

Further reading

Reference Books:

The Advertiser Annual and *The Creative Handbook*, both published by British Media Publications, Windsor Court, East Grinstead House, East Grinstead, West Sussex RH19 1XE.
Portfolio published by Marketing Publications Ltd, 22 Lancaster Gate, London W2 3LY.
Careers Encyclopedia published by Cassell Publishers Ltd, Artillery House, Artillery Row, London SW1P 1RT.

Periodicals

Campaign (weekly)
Marketing Week (weekly)
Marketing (weekly)